Written by Janice Deal and Marie Jones

Images from Shutterstock.com

Scripture quotations from *The Holy Bible, King James Version*.
Copyright © 1977, 1984, Thomas Nelson, Inc., Publishers.

Louis Weber, CEO
Publications International, Ltd.
8140 Lehigh Avenue
Morton Grove, IL 60053

ISBN: 978-1-64030-116-0

Manufactured in China.

8 7 6 5 4 3 2 1

POWERFUL PRAYERS
FOR WOMEN

Publications International, Ltd.

TABLE OF CONTENTS

Chapter 1

FIND STRENGTH

✴

*W*hat does it mean to be strong? Does it mean physical prowess or control over others? God has given us many kinds of strength, but the most important is the strength that comes from having a steadfast faith and a resilient spirit. With a foundation that is unshakable, we can then withstand any obstacle, challenge, or situation that comes our way.

And he poured the anointing oil upon Aaron's head and anointed him, to sanctify him.

—Leviticus 8:12

To be anointed in God's love is to be made into a powerful force for good. Be strong and go forward spreading light and love, for the world needs both now more than ever!

*L*ord God, I am about to throw in the towel!
I can't go on without your strength to get me over the
edge and into the light again. Help me remember why
I chose these goals and dreams to begin with, God.
Keep me strong to the finish!

*S*trengthen me, Lord Jesus. My confidence is fading fast.
Whenever I try to do things on my own steam, I mess up. So I'm
learning my lesson: I need your help. I understand that there's no
magic wand here. Your strength won't enable me to walk through
walls—unless we're talking about walls of my own prejudices or
fears. Help me face my challenges, attempt bold things, restore
long-strained relationships, and generally bring your presence
into my world. It's exciting to think about what that will look like,
but I know it's not my doing. It's all yours.

*God, I love this world,
for better or worse,
and I choose to fight for
what is good in it
every single day.*

It is easy to sit on the sidelines and fret about all that's wrong with the world. The stronger and more productive tactic, though, is to take the world for what it is—the good and the bad—and make a conscious choice to love it and be actively engaged. Find what is good in it, and cling to that. Fight to make the rest of it better. If we just sit on the sidelines and fret, we are part of the problem instead of being part of the solution.

O Lord, when I'm working on something that you're involved in, the work goes far better. The words flow as I write or the thoughts come as I speak. It's at those times that I'm sure I'm working not through my own strength but through yours. If you're in it, Lord, I can do it. If you aren't, I don't want to even try. I can do all things, but only through you. Thank you, Lord.

*G*reat God over all, I worship you today as my refuge and strength.
Thank you for your presence in my life. When I don't know where
to turn, I turn to you, and you welcome me. When I feel I can't go on,
you infuse me with extra energy. When I'm feeling all alone, you remind me
that you are always here, and you always care. Life has its share of troubles,
but you help me out of them. I praise and bless your holy name.

*L*ord, today, I will approach any objectionable situation with courage, even if—deep down— I am a little scared.

The bravest people are not those who never feared. In fact, those who had to lead in battle, fight rampant injustice, or stand up to horrible crimes likely felt more than a twinge of fear during their clashes. But they did not give in to the fear and let it stop them. They summoned something greater than the fear—their own courage. Courage comes from the deep belief of how life can and should be—and how good it is. The mere fact that they took action proves this, for why would someone bother taking action unless they thought the desired change would last and be worth the work and risk involved?

Before I formed thee in the belly I knew thee; and before thou camest forth out of the womb I sanctified thee.

—Jeremiah 1:5

Even before your birth, God instilled in you a strong spirit and an indomitable will to be a bright, shining light in the world.
Turn that light on and shine!
Let loose the joyful spirit that is you!

I am strong as an ox,
brave as a lion, and bold as a steer.
God's spirit within gives me the strength
to move mountains and the courage to go
the distance when others have given up.
I am powerful in his presence!

*W*e each face a different set of experiences, and this is what makes our life uniquely ours. This is an amazing thing to ponder—all the different experiences, all the different lives. Each experience we face makes us stronger and more prepared for the next experience. This is true even when at first an experience appears to be a negative one, whether it is a relatively small negative experience such as the frustration of getting lost on the way to our destination or a large negative experience, such as the death of a loved one. We face each experience with the strength and wisdom we have achieved through other past experiences. Each experience moves us forward and fills out the little spaces in us that need to be filled out. And then, voilà! We are who we were meant to be.

Lord, today I will not shrink from any experience. With you by my side, I know I can handle anything that comes my way because I have been formed from all my past experiences.

I've always tried to be a strong Christian, Lord. I've tried to live a disciplined life that others would admire. I hoped I'd be a positive influence, someone that others could turn to for advice or support. But somewhere along the line, my strength turned into pride. I started thinking only of myself and my image, and I stopped relying on you. Now I need your help in sorting this out. I humbly place myself in your service. It's not all about me anymore. It's about your power, your wisdom, and your plan. Teach me humility, Lord. Teach me trust.

O Lord, nothing drains us of our strength more completely than grief. But in times of sorrow, you come alongside us and give us strength to do things we never thought possible. Thus distraught family members are able to make final arrangements, deliver eloquent eulogies, and rise above their grief to do whatever needs to be done. We know that's your strength carrying us in those times, Lord. The promises in your Word give us hope. Your grace abounds in a special way to those who mourn. We praise you for your mercy, Lord. We thank you for your strength.

I can be afraid, but God gives me strength to act anyway. I can be uncertain, but God gives me a foundation that is firm and unyielding to stand upon.

By faith Noah, being warned of God of things not seen as yet, moved with fear, prepared an ark to the saving of his house; by the which he condemned the world, and became heir of the righteousness which is by faith.

—Hebrews 11:7

*L*ord, your love gives me all the strength I need to accomplish anything. Knowing that you deem me worthy of your love is the foundation of my entire faith. Understanding that you won't ever stop loving me is my shelter from the storms of life that challenge my peace and serenity. I know that I am always going to be loved no matter what I do, even when I don't always do the right thing. And that knowing fuels the desire to try to do the right thing, even when it is the harder thing to do. You have deemed me worthy. Now let me live up to that worthiness. Amen.

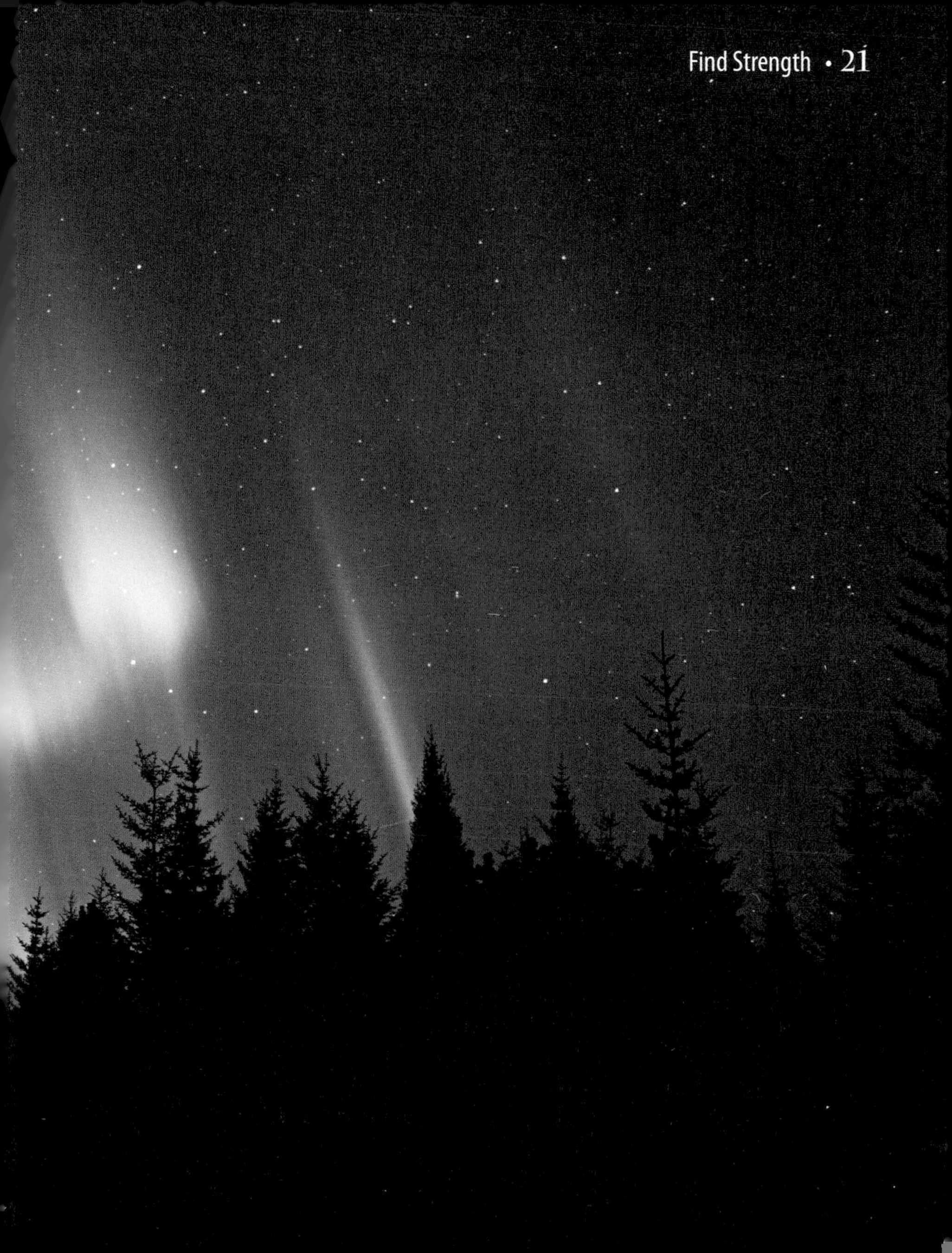

Be of good courage, and let us play the men for our people, and for the cities of our God: and the Lord do that which seemeth him good.

—2 Samuel 10:12

When the night is dark and cold, and the days promise little rest, be strong, because God has made you a promise of a mighty kingdom on the other side. Work hard, keep moving, and never let others derail you from your mission.

*G*od, there are times when I act small in the world because I'm afraid to get out of my comfort zone. I'm scared of looking foolish, or failing terribly and letting people down. Yet, you've given me talents and abilities and I long to use them for good in the world. Help me, God, to find that courageous lion within me, and to go forward with trust and inner strength, knowing that whatever comes up, you'll help me through it. I pray for your will to be done in my life, and for the fearlessness that comes from having you as my rock and my foundation. Let me shine my light, God, and help me not play it safe and miss out on the incredible experiences you have in store for me. Amen.

God made me a woman and God made me strong. I can be a mother, a lover, a friend, a sister, a daughter, and a caring and compassionate leader. I can do anything with God's presence as my power. I can be anything with God at my side!

Heavenly Father, I seek the nourishment that comes from true inner strength. I know that food fuels the body, but my spirit needs the fuel of deep and abiding peace and the understanding that I'm never alone in the world. With you, Father, I have that foundation of strength to feed me from the inside out. I'm able to go forth and face any challenge and overcome any obstacle. I ask that you continue to nourish me with resilience, fortitude, and faith.

*D*ear Lord, when I lean on you, I know that I'm leaning on a column of strength that will never fall down or waver. I may be uncertain and doubtful at times, but when I rest in your love, there's only certainty and faith. My belief may be tested at times, but my faith remains strong at its core. When I turn to you, Lord, I find a wellspring of pure, refreshing water to quench the thirsts of my body, mind, and soul. From that wellspring, I'm made whole and powerful like a column of solid rock that's able to withstand the strongest winds. Thank you, Lord.

*O*ne of my all-time favorite sayings is, "Do it anyway."
What does this mean? Well, for starters, we all have a tough life at
times. So what? Do we collapse by the side of the road and just give
up? Of course not. In some small way, we "do it anyway" every single
day. My joints ache some days, but I still go about my day with God's
help. Some months there's little money for groceries, but I still get
creative and put food on the table. We all do difficult things,
and each one makes us stronger.

God, today I will tell myself, "I am strong; I can do hard things,"—
and I will really believe it! You believe in me, so I have no
excuse not to believe in myself.

Thank you, God, for never forsaking me, whether times are good or bad. In my life I have encountered all manner of people: lifelong friends, false friends, family who comforted me in my cradle and then stood beside me as I grew. But life brings change again and again. Friends move; death might take our loved ones; fair-weather relationships fade in the face of adversity or simply with time; children grow and, with the wings we gave them, leave our homes to make their own rich lives. These changes can be difficult: sad, disappointing, or even scary. As I grow older, I sometimes fear change and the loss it can bring. Help me to remember that you are always there for me: a rock, a friend, and a comfort all the days of my life.

There shall not any man be able to stand before thee all the days of my life: as I was with Moses, so I will be with thee: I will not fail thee, not forsake thee.
—Joshua 1:5

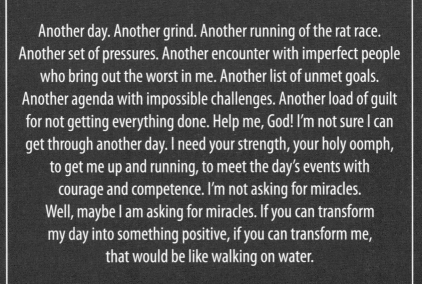

Another day. Another grind. Another running of the rat race. Another set of pressures. Another encounter with imperfect people who bring out the worst in me. Another list of unmet goals. Another agenda with impossible challenges. Another load of guilt for not getting everything done. Help me, God! I'm not sure I can get through another day. I need your strength, your holy oomph, to get me up and running, to meet the day's events with courage and competence. I'm not asking for miracles. Well, maybe I am asking for miracles. If you can transform my day into something positive, if you can transform me, that would be like walking on water.

*G*od, today I ask for strength—not for myself, but for others I care about. There are couples that need strength to get past some conflict in their relationships. Cover them with your overwhelming love. There are teenagers, still figuring out who they are, who need strength to withstand temptation. Shore up their souls. There are single parents working night and day to care for their families. Guard their health and refresh their energy. There are senior citizens who need strength to do the things they easily used to do. Give them grace to live mightily for you. All around me are people with emotional wounds and spiritual struggles, those who feel ill-equipped and overwhelmed. Support them with your power for your eternal glory.

$\mathcal{I}$ have always been a social drinker. Shy by nature, havir of wine helps me relax and feel more comfortable in social But lately I've noticed that I've begun to rely on a drink to unwind after work, or to gear up for a stressful encounter. When I made the decision to cut back, I was surprised and dismayed to discover how dependent I've become on alcohol to fill an emotional need. I think the best path for me is abstinence. Now that I no longer can rely on alcohol to "take off the edge," each day is a struggle.

Lord, please give me the strength to persevere in eschewing alcohol. I know my health and well-being will benefit. I thank you for your grace.

$\mathcal{I}$ am enduring a dark period, God. Alzheimer's disease ravages my beloved father, and I must assist him and my mother while I try to raise my own three children with strength, patience, and joy. Some nights I lie awake, filled with fear that my little family will not survive this next chapter—one of many "Sandwich Generation" families with children and parents to care for. God, help me remain faithful to the promise that with you, nothing is impossible, even if I can't see through it for myself.

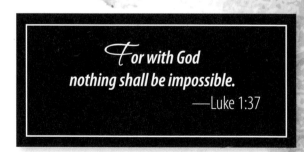

$\mathcal{F}$or with God
nothing shall be impossible.
—Luke 1:37

Lord, my heart aches for my friend, who is undergoing chemo-therapy. How it saps her energy, Lord. Sometimes it seems the cure is more devastating than the disease. Stay close to her in this time of healing, Lord. Bring her comfort, and fill her with the knowledge that she can find hope in you. I know you will lend her the strength she needs to get through this trying time.

Lord, please be my strength. When I am scared, please make me brave. When I am unsteady, please bring your stability to me. I look to your power for an escape from the pain. I welcome your comfort.

Chapter 2

BRING A FRIEND

✴

God puts friends in our lives to comfort us, support us, and share our burdens during dark times. And groups of friends can be powerful, indeed: Carrie, a single mom of two who lost her consulting job during an economic downturn, still remembers the solace provided by the prayer circle at her community church as she interviewed for a new position. "I knew others were thinking of me and praying for me," she shares. "It gave me strength."

*And Elijah said unto Elisha, Tarry here,
I pray thee; for the Lord hath sent me
to Bethel. And Elisha said unto him,
As the Lord liveth, and as thy soul liveth,
I will not leave thee.
So they went down to Bethel.*

—2 Kings 2:2

Knowing she needs encouragement, I pray for my friend, Lord. Lifting my heart to you on her behalf, may I not fail, either, to reach my hand to hers—just as you are holding mine.

*G*od gives us strength to go with our friends and share their burdens and responsibilities. When my friend and mentor Diane needed to travel to a cancer clinic in another city, I felt called to accompany her. I could not change her diagnosis, but I could be there, as a friend and companion, as she has been there for me these many years.

Dear God, thank you for the powerful gift of friendship. May I tap into your strength to be steadfast and true to my friends; as Elisha accompanied Elijah, may I walk beside my friends in good times and bad.

*Forbearing one another,
and forgiving one another,
if any man have a quarrel against any:
even as Christ forgave you,
so also do ye.*

—Colossians 3:13

Being a friend means that you need to reach out. Is there someone you can think of who needs to know that you are there for them—that you are a friend who cares? Pray for the spirit of friendship to so light up your life that you'll radiate this brightness to someone who needs you.

*G*od empowers us to forgive one another.
Natalie and her oldest friend Greta had
a falling out when Natalie got wind of the fact
that Greta had shared, with a mutual friend,
something Natalie had told Greta in confidence.
Though Greta's apology was sincere, Natalie's
confidence in their friendship was shaken.
Prayer and meditation helped Natalie talk
honestly with Greta about what had transpired,
and move forward with a relationship
that was essentially strong.

**Dear God, friendship can be a grounding
touchstone in this life. Just as you love and
forgive us, may I love and forgive others,
thus deepening the bonds of friendship.**

$\mathcal{W}$hen twelve-year-old Melissa found herself suddenly courted by the "cool girls" in her middle school, she began to ignore an old friend, Lily. Lily called her out on it, but Melissa's new friends laughed and said Lily wasn't worth Melissa's time. Feeling torn and unhappy, Melissa talked to her mom, who encouraged her to talk to God; in the quiet of home and prayer, Melissa saw the situation, and her steadfast friend, with clarity.

Dear God, a good friend lets us know when we've done wrong. May I be open to words of constructive criticism, shared by those who love me; may I see false platitudes for what they are.

$\mathcal{F}$*aithful are the wounds of a friend; but the kisses of an enemy are deceitful.*
—Proverbs 27:6

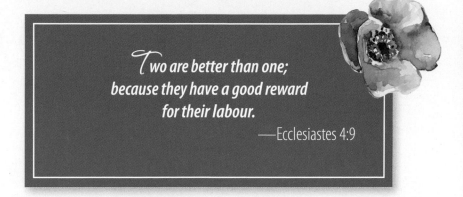

*Two are better than one;
because they have a good reward
for their labour.*

—Ecclesiastes 4:9

Terri's elderly mom, who has been struggling to keep up her house, is preparing the home for sale, and Terri offered to help with yard work. After one day of working the large, overgrown property, Terri confessed to a friend that she was feeling overwhelmed. Her friend not only offered to help, but showed up with her two cheerful sons in tow. "Working together, we had the yard in shape within a day!" Terri enthused. "It was fun!"

**Dear Lord, you put friends in my life, and I thank you.
Working together, my friends and I can move mountains.
Many together can accomplish much, and there is joy in the sharing!**

Henceforth I call you not servants; for the servant knoweth not what his lord doeth: but I have called you friends; for all things that I have heard of my Father I have made known unto you.

—John 15:15

God wants trusted friends for us. One of the things Doreen appreciates about her long-standing friendship with Karen is that the two can be open with one another. "I share anything with Karen," Doreen says. "When I went through my divorce, I was very angry, and Karen was someone I could talk to without censoring myself. She does not judge me. She knows my weaknesses as well as my strengths, and she *still* loves me!"

Dear Lord, may I follow the example of Jesus and share openly and completely with trusted friends.

*L*ife can be lonely. When Sarah's husband was offered a job in Seattle, the couple decided to take the plunge and relocate. Sarah scored a job in their new city, too, but adjusting to the move has been challenging. She misses her group of friends; one night, talking to her sister Ginny on the phone, Sarah felt near tears. "I'm here," Ginny said. "Just a phone call away. And remember, God is your friend, too. He's always there."

Dear God, you are my friend, always.

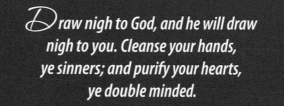

*D*raw nigh to God, and he will draw nigh to you. Cleanse your hands, ye sinners; and purify your hearts, ye double minded.

—James 4:8

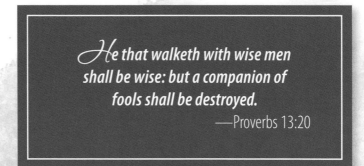

He that walketh with wise men shall be wise: but a companion of fools shall be destroyed.
—Proverbs 13:20

At Hannah's first job out of college, she quickly connected with a group of seemingly fun-loving women. But Hannah soon realized that gossip and drama characterized these friendships, and after some soul-searching, distanced herself from the group. It was only then she met quiet Liz, a fellow reader who invited Hannah to join her book club. Through Liz, Hannah has met a group of friends who share similar passions and ways of being in the world.

**Dear Lord, you put friends in my life to guide me.
May I surround myself with positive people
who help me to grow and be my best self.**

I answered the phone the other day. "Can Pat come out to play?" It was my best friend, wanting me to take a walk with her at a local park. I was in the middle of a project, and I really wanted to focus on finishing it. I sensed something in her voice, though, so I set my work aside. We chatted as we traversed the wooden walkway with dense Florida foliage and the Intracoastal Waterway in the background. But then she began to touch on more serious family problems. I listened, nodding and asking questions here and there. She talked and talked for a couple more miles. I was there for her, and I am mighty glad of it.

Lord, today I will call my friend who wants me to attend a class with her. I'll go, although vegetarian cooking is not really my thing. Who knows, perhaps I'll be healthier for it and perhaps she'll agree to take that Italian cooking class with me next year.

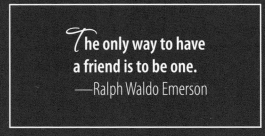

The only way to have
a friend is to be one.
—Ralph Waldo Emerson

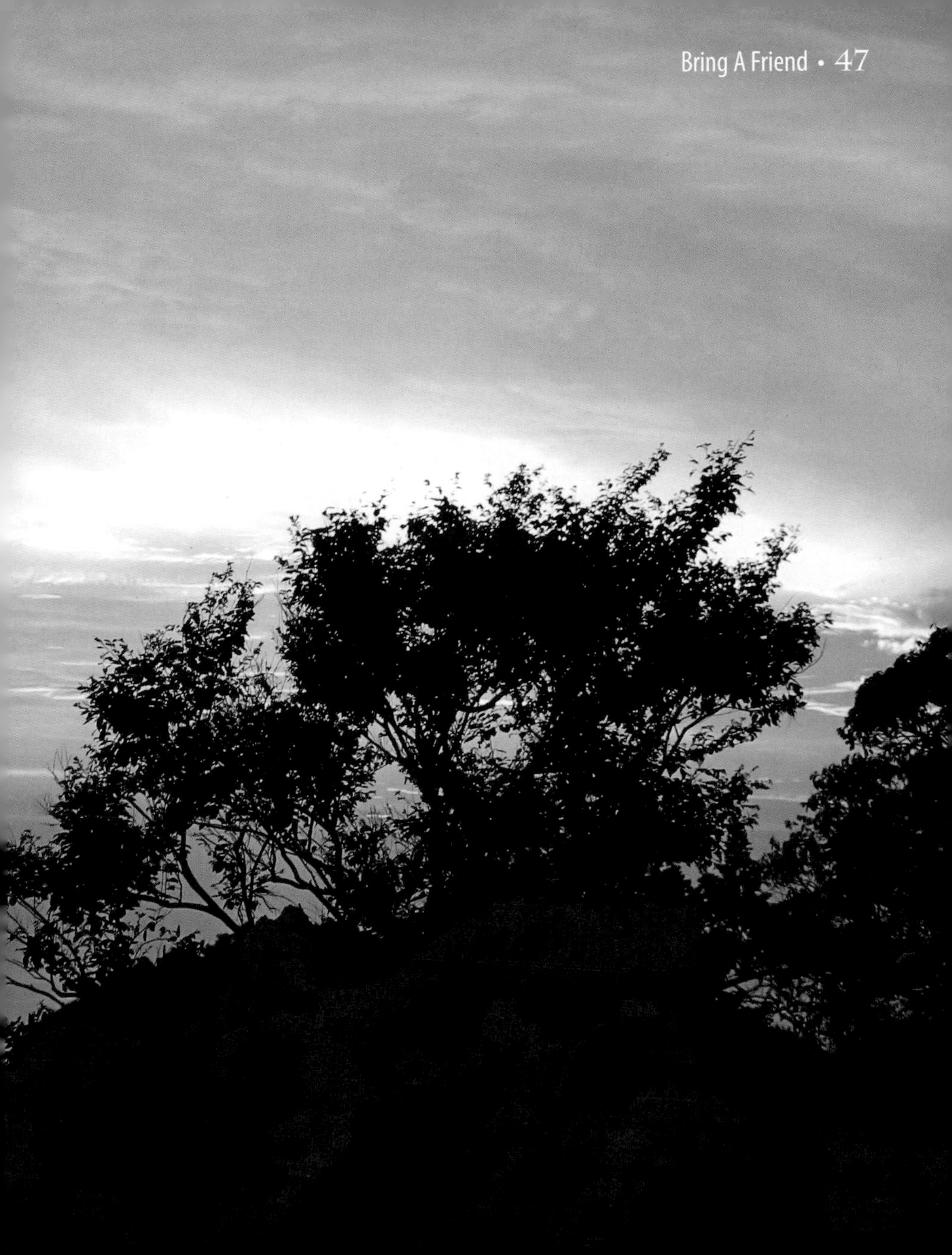

*C*helsea was blindsided when she learned she had breast cancer, but she and her husband have a strong network of friends who helped with cooking, babysitting, and cleaning during what proved to be a grueling schedule of chemotherapy and radiation. Seven years later, Chelsea is a cancer survivor—and grateful. "My friends had my back; I'll never forget that. They are stellar people, and I try to demonstrate, in my words and actions, how much they mean to me."

Dear God, may I treat my friends with love and honor.

*B*e kindly affectioned one to
another with brotherly love;
in honour preferring one another.
—Romans 12:10

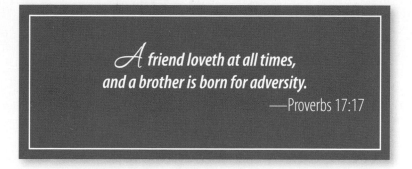

A friend loveth at all times,
and a brother is born for adversity.

—Proverbs 17:17

Renee's grandmother would say, "Welcome challenging times, and see who your friends are." Renee experienced that first hand when she became caregiver for her ailing dad. Over time, she learned who thought of her friendship as a priority. Some relationships faded because Renee's schedule was no longer as flexible. It was painful to realize that not all her friendships were as close as she'd thought, but looking back now, she appreciates—and celebrates—the friends who stuck by her.

God, thank you for those friends who love and
support us through hard times.

*Where no counsel is,
the people fall: but in the multitude
of counselors there is safety.*

—Proverbs 11:14

Mandy has always prided herself on her independence. But when buying a new home, she sought the advice of trusted friends: Ken, who works in construction and could spot structural issues, and Denise, who has a good head for finance and helped Mandy navigate the paperwork. With their support, she found a solid house at a price she could afford. "It's hard for me to rely on others," Mandy confessed. "But my friends helped me make a wise choice."

Dear Lord, grant me the humility to seek—and listen to!—the counsel of others. Grant me the wisdom to surround myself with wise friends.

> *And it came to pass, when he had made an end of speaking unto Saul, that the soul of Jonathan was knit with the soul of David, and Jonathan loved him as his own soul.*
>
> —1 Samuel 18:1

Saundra was nervous about starting college, and when she met her new roommate, she was filled with trepidation. A bookish, shy girl, Saundra felt intimidated by Claire, an artist with dyed blue hair who carried herself with confidence. In fact, the two became fast friends, despite—or maybe because of—their differences. "I'm a more well-rounded person, thanks to my friendship with Claire," Saundra says now. "And I think she'd say the same."

Dear God, David was an enemy of Saul—and yet Saul's own son Jonathan became David's close friend. Please help me to remember that you can unite even unlikely people in friendship.

ℒast summer I started bicycling regularly for my health. One day late in August I jumped a curb too exuberantly, wiped out, and broke my leg. Fortunately, I work from home, so my schedule was not too affected during my recuperation time. And yet, because I am by nature an active person, the limitations of my injury—not to mention the bulky cast—put a real cramp in my style. I'll confess that some days I felt down. My good friends Dave and Sara were a lifeline during this time. They'd stop by to watch movies, bring in dinner, or just hang out. We laughed a lot during these visits and I invariably found that after they looked in on me, my mood soared and I felt better overall. Long after my leg has healed, I remember their kindness with gratitude. Lord, thank you for the friends and loved ones who uplift me. Just as exercise, being joyful is good for my health!

𝒜 merry heart doeth good like a medicine: but a broken spirit drieth the bones.
—Proverbs 17:22

A faithful friend is an image of God.
—French Proverb

Dear Lord, my closest friends are a reprieve for my soul. Their acceptance sets me free to be myself. Their unconditional love forgives my failings. Thank you for these people who are a reflection of your love in my life. Help me be a friend who will lay down my life in such loving ways.

$\mathcal{W}$hen I was a girl, my mom used to talk about "refilling the well," by which she meant the joy she took in being with people who filled her up—who restored her. I thought of her expression last week, when I had lunch with an old classmate; when she and I parted, I was struck by how being with this friend energized rather than depleted me. She is a calm, spiritual person, and our times together never fail to leave me feeling uplifted. Our conversations are wide-ranging and thoughtful, and my friend is a person with whom I feel comfortable sharing my spiritual musings. She and I challenge one another; we don't always agree, but our relationship is such that we inspire one another to learn and grow.

Lord, may I remember the importance of developing relationships with other believers, whose fellowship and spiritual life can help to deepen my faith.

$\mathcal{A}$nd they continued stedfastly in the apostles' doctrine and fellowship, and in breaking of bread, and in prayers.
—Acts 2:42

For if they fall, the one will lift up his fellow: but woe to him that is alone when he falleth; for he hath not another to help him up.

—Ecclesiastes 4:10

Lord, so many times when I've been down, time with a good friend has lifted me up again and helped me to face my circumstances with a better attitude. Sometimes that friend is my best friend—my husband—but other times it's one of my precious female friends who seems to intuitively know the precise advice I need. Thank you, Lord, for dear friends. May I be such a friend to others.

*Friendships, like gardens, must be nourished
and cultivated if they are to flourish and thrive.
Take time to pull the weeds, turn the soil,
and plant new seeds. Then enjoy the
beauty of this love you have created.*

God, today I will find time to reflect on my
friendships. If there is someone I need to forgive
(or if I need forgiveness from another) I will
make amends, then bask in the peace.

If you have one true friend,
you have more than your share.
—Thomas Fuller

Dear God, today I grew frustrated with my old friend and said some hurtful things. I will pray on it and hope for her forgiveness, and I have faith that you'll help us to mend our friendship. When we find people we love and wish to include in our lives, we must work to hang on to them. Help me to gain compassion and understanding as I resolve the situation.

Happy is the house that shelters a friend.

—Ralph Waldo Emerson

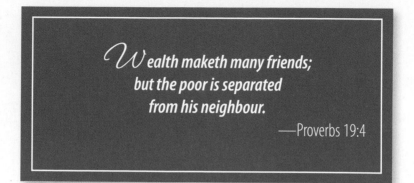

Wealth maketh many friends; but the poor is separated from his neighbour.

—Proverbs 19:4

Lord, if only everyone could adopt your law of love as our neighbors have. I thank you for sending good friends who are always ready to provide our children with shelter and a cookie in any emergency, to lend equipment or advice, to offer an occasional ride or a meal—to help out in any way they can. Where would we be without their valued assistance?

I am grateful for their kindness, their willingness, and their generous spirits. Bless these loving people, Father, who are your hands reaching out to care for us. Please make me a good neighbor to them, and may I find many opportunities to return your love by helping them when they are in need.

They helped every one his neighbour;
and every one said to his brother,
Be of good courage.

—Isaiah 41:6

I thank you for the healing power of friends and for the positive emotions friendship brings. Thank you for sending companions to me so we can support and encourage one another and share our joys and sorrows. My friends represent for me your presence and friendship here on Earth. Please keep them in your care, Father. We need each other, and we need you. Amen.

$\mathcal{B}$eing an adult—perhaps more specifically being a spiritual adult—does not mean that we have to be dull or unadventurous. I was recently happily reminded of this fact when I met a man at my church who embodies the spirit of adventure. Like me, Matt is probably in his late 50s. Like me, he lost his spouse to terminal illness. I have admittedly become stuck in my ways since becoming a widow five years ago. Meeting Matt has been like a shot of sunshine. He is taking lessons to earn a motorcycle license. He loves woodworking and has sold a few pieces of his handmade furniture online. Though he still holds down a full-time job, Matt enjoys volunteering at a nearby animal shelter, an effort that has brought two tabby cats into his life. I don't know where our friendship will lead, but I can say that my relationship with Matt has broadened my horizons and filled me with joy.

God, thank you for reminding me that you want us to be happy.

Chapter 3

HOLD STEADY

Dear Lord, help me find my footing again. I'm feeling really shaky lately, and I long for that assurance that I never truly walk alone. I ask for the courage to move past these scary times and the fortitude to keep on going even when I feel like giving in on myself and on everything and everyone around me. I know, Lord, that you will never give up on me. Help me walk the straight and narrow path again.

For his anger endureth but a moment; in his favour is life: weeping may endure for a night, but joy cometh in the morning.
—Psalm 30:5

Help me grieve and go on—go on in a new way you will reveal to me, Lord, as I make my faltering way as far as I can. Hold me while I name and mourn all that I have lost, weeping like the abandoned child I feel I am. Then, in time and with you to steady me, I can focus on what I have left.

*D*ear God, I could use a steadying hand today. My life seems like a roller-coaster, filled with so many ups and downs it's making my head spin. I could use a fortifying courage today. I'm being dealt so many lousy cards to play. Help me keep the faith, God, and stay in your will for me. Amen.

*L*et us hold fast the profession
of our faith without wavering;
(for he is faithful that promised).
—Hebrews 10:23

Dear God, thank you for giving me a powerful foundation of faith in my life. From this foundation, I am able to build so much peace, harmony, and happiness, just by trusting in you and in your unceasing guidance. I walk in gratitude daily for the miraculous way having faith in your will seems to work. No matter what is going on around me, if I stand in faith, I stand strong. I pray that I always have this trust in your will to depend on, especially when my own will leads me astray. I pray that my life be a testament to others of the wonders that happen when we put our faith in you, God, where it belongs. Amen.

God, it's hard to hold the course when so many obstacles are thrown in my way. I ask your help navigating through my days with a powerful faith and a steadfast trust that I can do this thing called life, and do it with grace and joy. Help me stay the course!

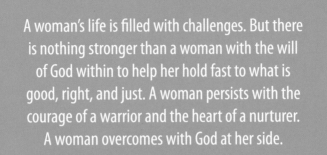

A woman's life is filled with challenges. But there is nothing stronger than a woman with the will of God within to help her hold fast to what is good, right, and just. A woman persists with the courage of a warrior and the heart of a nurturer. A woman overcomes with God at her side.

If ye have faith as a grain of mustard seed, ye shall say unto this mountain, Remove hence to yonder place; and it shall remove; and nothing shall be impossible unto you.

—Matthew 17:20

Hold fast to your belief in yourself, and God's belief in you. Do this one thing, and you can do anything, achieve anything! Never waver in trusting that you are being guided and directed. Go for it!

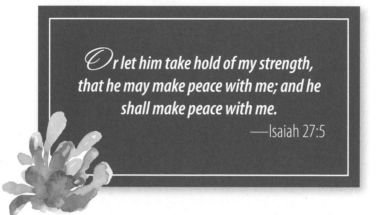

Or let him take hold of my strength, that he may make peace with me; and he shall make peace with me.

—Isaiah 27:5

As the seasons change and the exterior world becomes a different place, we can find the strength, power, and guidance we need by staying focused on the steady, unchangeable, infinite center within.

I may not understand your ways, God, or what your plans are for me, but I trust you. I know you have my best interest always at heart, and you won't lead me astray. My trust in your will acts like a lighthouse beacon guiding me safely to shore.

> *Trust in the Lord with all thine heart; and lean not unto thine own understanding.*
> —Proverbs 3:5

*Hearken, my beloved brethren,
Hath not God chosen the poor of this
world rich in faith, and heirs of the
kingdom which he hath promised to
them that love him?*

—James 2:5

Father, when I don't have another ounce of strength to give, you give me gallons of love to fuel my spirit. When I think I can't continue, you push me further and steady my steps. Thank you, God.

*L*ast year, an old college friend called with the devastating news that after twenty-five years of marriage, her husband had admitted to a long-standing affair and asked for a divorce. My friend had felt secure in her husband's love and was blindsided by this betrayal. In the months since, she has taken comfort in the community of her church, and found solace in her faith. "It's true that sometimes people disappoint us," she told me recently. We'd met for lunch, and though she spoke wryly, she looked and sounded better than she had in months. "But God is always faithful to us." I was struck by her words, and on the walk home pondered the resilience that grows when we know someone has our back.

Dear Lord, help me to remember that you are a steady constant in my life, in times of joy and adversity.

*G*od is faithful, by whom ye were called unto the fellowship of his Son Jesus Christ our Lord.
—1 Corinthians 1:9

*G*od, when I feel unsteady, you alone provide the firm ground beneath my feet. Illuminate my path so that I am always living in your will and not from my own limited ego. Show me how to be the best I can be under all circumstances, good and bad.

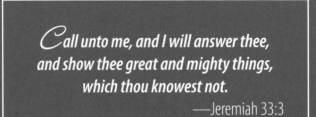

*C*all unto me, and I will answer thee, and show thee great and mighty things, which thou knowest not.

—Jeremiah 33:3

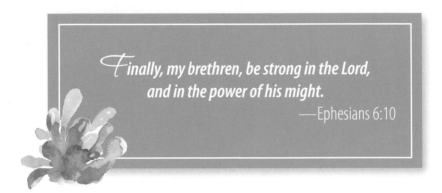

Finally, my brethren, be strong in the Lord, and in the power of his might.

—Ephesians 6:10

When the world rocks you off your center, hold fast to God to bring you back to harmony and balance. When life pulls the rug out from under you, jump and land square on the foundation of God's love for you. When all seems lost, God will help you find your way again.

The Lord is my light and my salvation; whom shall I fear? the Lord is the strength of my life; of whom shall I be afraid?

—Psalm 27:1

O Lord, try as we might to stay grounded in faith in the face of uncertainty, fear sometimes grabs hold of us. We become mired in a bog of "what ifs." What if the test comes back positive? What if this is the end of their marriage? What if the baby comes too early? All the struggles of life can strike fear in our hearts. But you, O Lord, are our God! There isn't a situation or a person that should cause us to fear when we place our trust in you. Thank you, Lord, for rescuing us from fear.

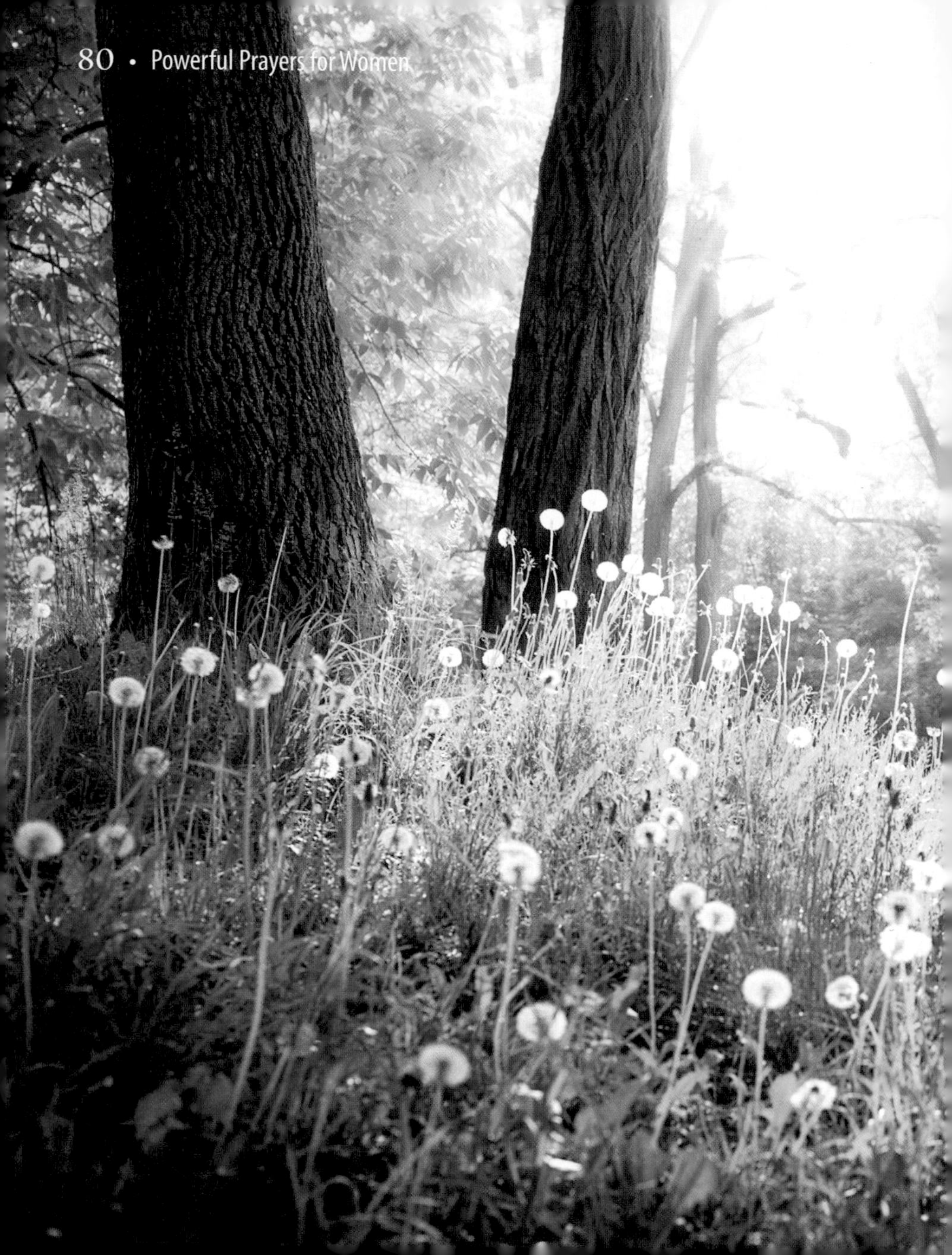

Guide me, pathfinding God, for I'm an aerialist leaping from bar to bar. For seconds, I'm holding neither old nor new: It's impossible to grasp a second bar while holding the first. Parents understand. We can't embrace kids' growth while requiring them to stay the same. Help me teach my kids how to swing on their bars—have standards, goals, and a living faith. Steady me as I help them soar, for holding them back says I think they can't. No matter what today is like, tomorrow will be different. Help me, and the kids, live gracefully in between.

Help us, O Lord our God; for we rest on thee, and in thy name we go against this multitude. O Lord, thou art our God; let no man prevail against thee.

—2 Chronicles 14:11

Sometimes the "multitude" we face is a multitude of pain, a multitude of trouble, a multitude of opposition from others, or a multitude of sadness. When it feels as though there is a multitude of something that is too big for us, threatening to distress us, what can we do? There is only one who is bigger and more powerful than anyone or anything else in life. Let us remember today that our God is for us, and his power is greater than that of any multitude.

My God, in you I stand today against the multitude that would seek to discourage my faith. In every circumstance that threatens to overwhelm me, please grant me your peace as you exercise your power to protect me.

*G*od, teach me to not fear adversity. It is a mother's knee-jerk reaction to protect her children from all trials, but one cannot travel through life without reversals of fortune. Help me to accept and face challenges not only to myself but to my children. My kids will face unkindness; they will face unfairness, loss, and even cruelty in their life's journey. God, help me to remember that adversity breeds character—that we cannot necessarily control what happens to us but we can control our response to it. Grant me the strength to respond to adversity with grace, and please guide me as I give my children the tools to greet life's vicissitudes with faith in you, and with courage.

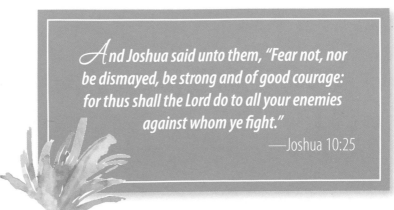

And Joshua said unto them, "Fear not, nor be dismayed, be strong and of good courage: for thus shall the Lord do to all your enemies against whom ye fight."

—Joshua 10:25

There is only one happiness and that is to cease worrying about the things which are beyond the power of your own will.

—Epictetus

So much of our time is wasted worrying about things that are beyond our control. The economy? Vote your conscience and find and maintain the best job you can, and you have done your part. Poverty? Don't overindulge yourself and regularly donate time or money to a local soup kitchen or food depository, and your part is done. Inconsiderate drivers? Send positive vibes their way (they obviously need them!) and move on.

God, today I will mind my part in this life, and it will be enough. You can handle the rest.

$\mathscr{L}$ord, it nearly drives me to distraction to hear my children arguing over trifles. Each wants what the other has. When one says something, the other contradicts. I try, but there seems to be no way to avoid these battles. I need your steadying hand, Father, to help me cope. Only you can calm the waters of discontent that swirl around them and plant peace within their hearts. Soothe us with the balm of your Holy Spirit so my children can live together in pleasant harmony.

Although our eyes should always be turned above toward God, sometimes we can do with a reminder of God's work just a little bit closer to home. The faith of others can serve as a reminder or an inspiration to strengthen our own faith. Just as we should provide encouragement to others, we can draw on others to help steady ourselves.

If you want your dreams to bear big fruit, you must be patient enough to let the buds grow into fullness, even if it feels like it's taking forever. Remember, God's timing is not your timing. Stick to it. Don't give up just before you get that bold breakthrough!

Everything around me keeps changing, Lord. Nothing lasts. My relationships with others are different than they were before. I started to feel as if there is nothing sure and steady on which I can depend. Then I remembered your ever-present, unchanging love. Through these transitions, your love gives me courage and hope for the future. Amen.

*A*nd straightway the father of the
child cried out, and said with tears, Lord,
I believe; help thou mine unbelief.

—Mark 9:24

I need to believe beyond the present darkness,
for it threatens to stop me in my tracks. Steady me, God
of infinite resources, as I collect my beliefs like candles
to light and move through this dark tunnel of doubt and
uncertainty. Inspire me to add new truths as they reveal
themselves in my life. Along the way, help my unbelief.

I recently changed jobs. For many years, I'd worked in a doctor's office and for most of the time, the pros of that situation outweighed the cons. I enjoyed flexible hours, a godsend when my elderly mother grew ill and needed more help. But my boss was never supportive and the pay was not ideal. When my mom passed away last year, I decided to look for a different position, and almost immediately found a new job. I am excited about this next chapter, but change can also be hard. During these first weeks at work, the learning curve has been steep and some nights I am tired and stressed.

Dear God, please live in my heart and help me to remain steadfast as I seek to learn, grow, and improve my situation and myself. Please remind me, on the days when my spirit flags, that you are always there.

Chapter 4

ONE STEP

*You don't need to run a marathon.
Just take one step at a time.
Go out in faith and let God guide you.
There is a season for everything,
and God has perfect timing.
Just listen and when he tells
you to move, move!*

So teach us to number our days, that we may apply our hearts unto wisdom.
—Psalm 90:12

I watch the days of my life fly by, always thinking of what I need to do tomorrow, next week, next month. God, help me to slow down and take it all one step at a time, and drink in every present moment, for those moments will never come again.

God, give me the patience to take this
thing called life one step at a time.
Stop me from rushing things and
demanding they happen in my time.
Give me the wisdom to allow them to
happen on your clock, not mine. Amen.

A journey of a thousand miles begins with one step.

—Chinese Proverb

Father, I pray today for a clear path, a strong wind at my back pushing me forward, and the courage of a lion to step into greatness. I am afraid and uncomfortable, but with you I can begin the journey of a thousand miles—with one bold step.

How much happier and at peace would
we be if we allowed God to order our days?
If we just focus on the promises of his love
for us, all else will fall into place accordingly,
without our exhausting effort!

> But seek ye first the kingdom of God,
> and his righteousness; and all these things
> shall be added unto you.
>
> —Matthew 6:33

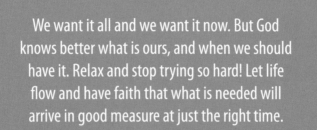

We want it all and we want it now. But God knows better what is ours, and when we should have it. Relax and stop trying so hard! Let life flow and have faith that what is needed will arrive in good measure at just the right time.

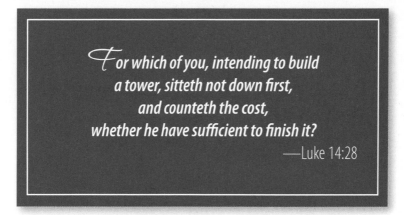

*For which of you, intending to build
a tower, sitteth not down first,
and counteth the cost,
whether he have sufficient to finish it?*
—Luke 14:28

The first step toward accomplishing any goal is to make a plan. Ask God to help you lay the blueprint for your dream, for he knows best the right tools to use, and the strongest materials to build with.

Usually, achieving big goals involves many small steps rather than one big leap. We must have patience and perseverance. When we call to mind the big feats in history, there were likely many points leading up to these achievements when the major players could have become discouraged and given up. If the end goal is worth it, we must do whatever it takes to achieve it. Lord, today I will contemplate my big goal and take at least one small step toward it.

God, today I will do something to improve the world around me, whether it's volunteering in some capacity, giving money to a reputable charity, or writing to my representative about a local issue. I pray that one step will lead me to take another.

*L*ord, give me the faith to take the next step, even when I don't know what lies ahead. Give me the assurance that even if I stumble and fall, you'll pick me up and put me back on the path. And give me the confidence that, even if I lose faith, you will never lose me.

I think most of us have attempted new things in different ways. It is true that when we face a task with confidence and tranquility, things tend to go more smoothly, while if we are afraid and approach something tentatively, our fears tend to get realized. If there is something we truly want to accomplish, we must begin by boldly taking that first step. Success in anything is truly an inside job. God, today I will not be afraid. What is there to lose? With you on my side, I will prevail.

When my dear husband died last year, many friends stepped forward, but some—even friends I hold dear— disappointed me by not being there for me as much as I might have hoped. Death is a frightening thing, my husband's death was untimely, and I tried to remember that people's lives are complex. Sometimes, I imagine, my expectations were simply too high. And yet it was painful for me to understand that some loved ones could not, for whatever reason, be there for me in my grief. It was only through prayer that I gained a measure of relief, perspective, and calm.

God, thank you for always being there to listen to me. With your help, I know I can move forward, one step at a time.

> And when ye stand praying, forgive, if ye have ought against any: that your Father also which is in heaven may forgive you your trespasses.
>
> —Mark 11:25

M any of us fall into the trap of putting things off. We'd like to have a job that pays better, presents more challenge, or offers more creativity, but we leave off doing much about it. We want to get fit and healthy, but we figure we'll "start tomorrow." We yearn for more companionship with others, but we wait for others to invite us over or make plans. Get something started right now. Make the first move toward your most desired goal. Lord, today if I find myself starting to daydream about something, I will make the first move to make it happen.

Dear God, help me create a new habit today. I want to wake up each morning and take one step forward toward my dreams. Just one. I want to build confidence and increase my courage, so that I'll soon be taking one giant leap forward.

I have such good intentions, Lord of promise,
but sometimes I slip in carrying them out.
Guide my actions so that they match my words
as I make footprints for my children to follow.
Make me worthy of being a pathfinder. Amen.

*W*hen I leave you behind and try to go about my day without your guidance, Lord, it's like groping around in the dark. I stub my heart on relational issues. I trip over my ego. I bump into walls of frustration. I fall down the steps of my foolish choices. How much better to seek the light of your presence first thing and enjoy the benefit of having you illuminate each step of my day!

*Casting all your care upon him;
for he careth for you.*

—1 Peter 5:7

I am the single mom of two teens. The last year has been challenging for me as a parent. My daughter has had a hard time adjusting to the rigors of high school academics, and my son has been testing boundaries when it comes to curfews and expectations at home. Some nights I am troubled by insomnia, and then the next day, I have a shorter fuse. Tempers flare. Dear Lord, please help me to remember to take one step at a time. You are there for me. You are the answer to my anxiety. Help me to parent with wisdom and rely on you, even when I feel stressed and uncertain.

*Thou art my hiding place and my shield:
I hope in thy word.*
—Psalm 119:116

Step into the future with
faith in your ability to
conquer the unknown.

*W*hat might we do today, if we brushed off any fears that surfaced? Doing something we fear is liberating and empowering. I remember the first time I tried snorkeling. It may not seem like much, but after nearly drowning in my youth, I lived with a terrible fear of water. I still vividly remember putting on the mask and snorkel and dipping my head into the water, only to quickly pull it out in a panic. But then I looked around at the lovely, serene sea, and I decided to give it one more try. I did, and today I count snorkeling and diving among my favorite pastimes. Lord, today I will attempt something I have avoided in the past. Perhaps I will apply for that dream job or sign up for a class that will bring me one step closer to it.

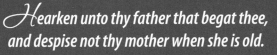

*Hearken unto thy father that begat thee,
and despise not thy mother when she is old.*

—Proverbs 23:22

*T*hroughout my life I have enjoyed many milestones: attaining a college degree, securing my first job, marriage, the birth of my two children, and just recently, seeing my relationship with my parents flip as they age and begin to rely on me as I once relied on them. Each life chapter has brought its joys and trials, and while it is my privilege to support my mom and dad, I confess that their new vulnerability sometimes fills me with fear, and on my worst days, resentment. My life is so full. My children, in high school now, still need me, perhaps more than ever as they face more adult challenges of their own. Sometimes I feel like there aren't enough hours in the day to work and make sure the needs of my loved ones are met. Sometimes I don't want to face or be present for the way my parents have aged. God, as I grow older and my life becomes more complicated, please help me to remember to always honor my mother and father. They remain my parents and have much to offer me. May I never forget them or shirk my responsibilities amid the everyday cares of working and parenting.

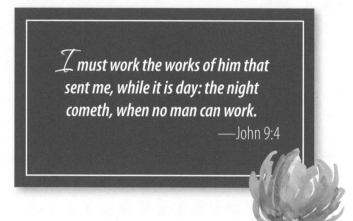

> *I must work the works of him that sent me, while it is day: the night cometh, when no man can work.*
>
> —John 9:4

My job is to do what God asks of me. That's it. I am not expected to go the full distance in one day. All God wants is for me to take that first step, and he will do the rest when he is ready.

*D*aily life is so full of duties and commitments that my dreams often take a backseat to my to-do list and to the demands of work and loved ones. Some nights I consider myself lucky if I have time to read a page of a book at night before I fall asleep, exhausted! But I know my dreams are always there on the periphery, waiting for me to make a move toward them. I need to make them more of a priority in my life. Lord, today I will reflect on what my highest aspirations are, and I will take one definite step toward one of them.

All I have to do is take the first step and God will meet me there. Together, we will walk the path and meet every challenge with courage. Together, we will find miracles waiting around every corner. Just one step...

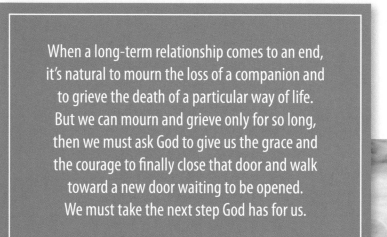

When a long-term relationship comes to an end, it's natural to mourn the loss of a companion and to grieve the death of a particular way of life. But we can mourn and grieve only for so long, then we must ask God to give us the grace and the courage to finally close that door and walk toward a new door waiting to be opened. We must take the next step God has for us.

*A*long this path of life, Lord Jesus, I've come to realize that no person can be to me what you are. There is a wide spectrum of disappointment I have experienced at the hands of others (including disappointments with myself). Some letdowns have been inadvertent and easy to forgive. Others have been intentional and mean-spirited, and I have struggled to leave these deeper hurts in your hands. But with you, Lord, there is perfect love and support, pure mercy and forgiveness. You are my source of unfailing companionship, and I'm deeply grateful that you walk beside me.

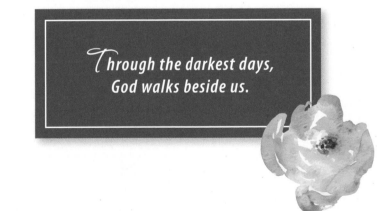

Through the darkest days,
God walks beside us.

The Lord is not slack concerning his promise, as some men count slackness; but is longsuffering to us-ward, not willing that any should perish, but that all should come to repentance.

—2 Peter 3:9

"Two steps forward, one step back." My mom, a physical therapist, sometimes says this to clients who feel discouraged about the long road to recovery. "But you'll get there," she always adds. Mom is a spiritual person, and she shared with me once that not only does she think her maxim applies to any process of self-improvement, it reminds her of God's faith in us. I was deeply struck by her observation! Self-improvement is a long haul, marked by setbacks and detours. And yet, God, you are always patient with me, and believe that I can better myself. Thank you for believing in my potential and efforts; I am bolstered by your patience and love.

$\mathcal{F}$rom time to time, we all act on faith, even if we don't recognizing it as such. Would a farmer plant his fields if he did not expect to reap a harvest in due time? Would a student attend classes and study if she did not believe it would further her life and career? Would we get up and go to work each day if we did not hope that by doing so we would accomplish something? Perhaps if we tap into faith more often and more deliberately, we will be moved to act with more purpose and conviction. Lord, today I will act upon something I believe in, even if I cannot yet see the end result.

Today is my new beginning, the past is over and done, however I got to this point, from here I can only move on. Though the road ahead may be rocky, and the future I cannot see, I'll walk with my head held high, with angels on each side of me. Today is my new beginning, and as I depart, I will pray, that God will bless my journey, and guide me each step of the way.

Chapter 5

LOOK AROUND

*When I follow God's will and do as he instructs me,
my direction becomes clear as I step out onto the path.
I look around and see his presence everywhere,
guiding me forward to where my spirit longs to be.
I see his signs showing me the way.*

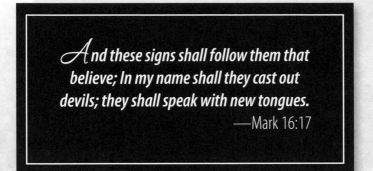

And these signs shall follow them that believe; In my name shall they cast out devils; they shall speak with new tongues.
—Mark 16:17

God, living in your grace empowers me to be the woman I was born to be. I look and listen for your guidance, and I move with gratitude in the direction that will help me achieve the great things you expect of me.

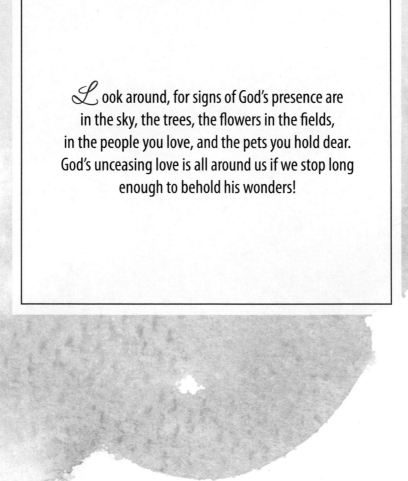

*L*ook around, for signs of God's presence are
in the sky, the trees, the flowers in the fields,
in the people you love, and the pets you hold dear.
God's unceasing love is all around us if we stop long
enough to behold his wonders!

> *et thine eyes look right on, and let thine eyelids look straight before thee.*
>
> —Proverbs 4:25

The wisdom and insight we need is often hidden in plain sight, right before our eyes, and under our very noses. God is always guiding us, if we stop and open our hearts and spirits to the still, small whisperings within us that point the way.

*W*hen you need a helping hand, look around
for the angels God has placed in your path.
Human angels come in the form of friends,
mentors, and even strangers with words meant
just for you to hear. Reach out, look, receive God's
blessings through his earthly angels.

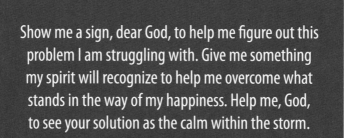

Show me a sign, dear God, to help me figure out this problem I am struggling with. Give me something my spirit will recognize to help me overcome what stands in the way of my happiness. Help me, God, to see your solution as the calm within the storm.

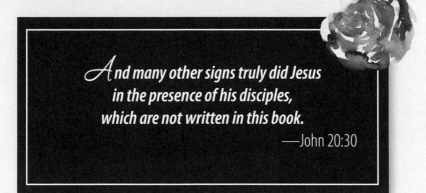

*And many other signs truly did Jesus
in the presence of his disciples,
which are not written in this book.*

—John 20:30

Sometimes, what we are looking for exists within us.
We love to look outside of ourselves for peace, joy,
and happiness. But those are gifts of God, and God
empowers us from within. Stop and turn inward,
and there you will find God.

I can only achieve so much without looking to those who have come before me. God has given me the gift of wisdom by placing people in my life who have the experience and insights I seek.

The keeper of the prison looked not to any thing that was under his hand; because the Lord was with him, and that which he did, the Lord made it to prosper.

—Genesis 39:23

*G*uidance is there, but you must look with your heart. Let go of what the mind and ego see, for it is not the truth. Follow where your heart leads, for it is led by the spirit of a loving and powerful God who wants what is best for you.

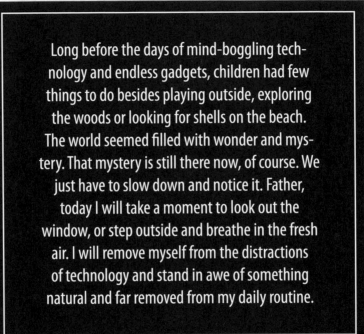

Long before the days of mind-boggling technology and endless gadgets, children had few things to do besides playing outside, exploring the woods or looking for shells on the beach. The world seemed filled with wonder and mystery. That mystery is still there now, of course. We just have to slow down and notice it. Father, today I will take a moment to look out the window, or step outside and breathe in the fresh air. I will remove myself from the distractions of technology and stand in awe of something natural and far removed from my daily routine.

I move through my days with a sense of purpose, but sometimes I am so consumed by the immediate to-dos that I forget to be open to—or even aware of—opportunities to help those around me. This week was no exception. My mind has been on a tight work deadline, and at night, I've been tackling a series of home organization projects. It was only when my husband sat me down and made me put my phone aside that I slowed down long enough for him to share that a close friend of ours has been battling depression. If I'd been paying attention, I might have seen the signals. This friend is usually good about staying in touch, but I hadn't heard from her in several months. "Why don't you give her a call?" was my husband's gentle suggestion. God, help me to be sensitive to those I love, and those in need. Jesus was responsive when he learned that Lazarus was sick; may I likewise show compassion to those around me.

> *T*herefore his sisters sent unto him,
> saying, Lord, behold,
> he whom thou lovest is sick.
> —John 11:3

Regardless of what the future holds, I'm savoring all sorts of wondrous things I've been too busy to notice before. A thousand daily marvels bring a smile to my face. Through your grace, Lord, rather than thinking how sad it is that I missed them before, I'm delighted to be seeing, doing them now. These small wonders energize me, and for that I'm thankful. It's never too late to be a joyful explorer.

> The real voyage of discovery lies not in seeking new landscapes but in having new eyes.
> —Marcel Proust

Lord, today I ask you to slow me down and open my ears and eyes so I will notice the needs of those around me. Too often I breeze by people with an offhand greeting but remain in a cocoon of my own concerns. I know many around me are hurting, Lord. Help me find ways to be of service.

*F*ear thou not; for I am with thee:
be not dismayed; for I am thy God:
I will strengthen thee; yea, I will help thee;
yea, I will uphold thee with the right hand
of my righteousness.

—Isaiah 41:10

My mom died of cancer when I was still in college. She was diagnosed with a brain tumor in the spring and was gone before Christmas. My dad was devastated and in his grief, withdrew from the world; he could not be there for us kids to lean on emotionally. It was a very difficult time in my life. What got me through was the support I received at the church in my college town. In what was probably the loneliest time in my life, I was nevertheless surrounded by love. Various members of the congregation invited me over for home-cooked meals or pizza-and-movie nights. These folks encouraged me that God was still there, and through their loving actions, I experienced God's grace. God is with us even when we feel alone.

Blessed be God, even the Father of our Lord Jesus Christ, the Father of mercies, and the God of all comfort; Who comforteth us in all our tribulation, that we may be able to comfort them which are in any trouble, by the comfort wherewith we ourselves are comforted of God.

—2 Corinthians 1:3–4

God of comfort, help me lift my eyes and look beyond myself. What people around me are in need of your consolation? Have you given me this difficult experience to equip me to help them? Are there other ailing people who will listen to me because I know what they're going through? Are there people visiting me who are troubled by worries and fears? Are there doctors and nurses who are overworked and desperately needing a moment of joy or a word of love? Show me these needs and how I can meet them.

*H*ow often do we lose perspective by focusing on the trivial, annoying details of life? I think most of us have had this experience: After a "bad" day, we catch sight of some natural beauty by happenstance and find ourselves magically renewed. Life is about focusing on the beautiful and the fulfilling and letting go of the silly and constraining.

The next time I find myself feeling overwhelmed, Lord, I will seek out nature and immerse myself in it for a half hour.

*R*est is not idleness, and to lie sometimes on the grass under trees on a summer's day, listening to the murmur of the water, or watching the clouds float across the sky, is by no means a waste of time.

—Sir John Lubbock

*W*e work on islands inside efficient cubes as small as a closet, as private as an elevator, and as cozy as a phone booth. Lord, give us the courage to peek around corners. We want to take down the walls a notch. It's not good for folks to live, or work, alone.

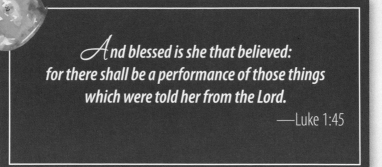

And blessed is she that believed:
for there shall be a performance of those things
which were told her from the Lord.
—Luke 1:45

Our relationships strengthen us. This came home to me the other day, when an exchange with a coworker left me feeling irresolute and unsettled. During my commute home, my stomach was in knots. I went over and over the disagreement in my head. It was hard to sort out whether I'd handled things with grace. When I got home and looked around, I found that my husband had started dinner; the warm atmosphere of love and regard unclenched my heart, and I was able to talk frankly about the day. My husband's nonjudgmental but clear-sighted perspective helped me sort how to remedy the situation. After we talked, we took a moment to pray together. God, thank you for reminding us of the importance of believing in you and in one another.

She is more precious than rubies: and all the things thou canst desire are not to be compared unto her.

—Proverbs 3:15

Life can be complicated; in the larger world we are challenged, sometimes on a daily basis, to be our best selves. Perhaps we don't see eye-to-eye with a coworker. Maybe we need to have a talk with a friend who has hurt us, even though we dislike confrontation. Maybe the sweet, adoring toddler we remember walking to preschool has morphed into a teen who is trying to individuate—but doesn't yet know how to do that in a mature or loving way? Though life's hurts can chip away at our spirits, God reminds us that each of us has value. May we never lose sight of the fact that God created us! May we never lose sight of our inherent worth.

The creative power within is your power to overcome any obstacle and break through any binding walls that keep you from your dreams. This power was given to you by the greatest of all creators, the one who created you, God. Just look around at the amazing beauty and diversity of the world you live in, and you will never again doubt that God supports your creative endeavors.

We all have numerous resources from which to share. Having a "generous spirit" does not mean simply giving money. Time is another precious commodity, and generous volunteers enable many organizations to function well: hospitals, schools, missions, animal shelters, community centers, nursing homes, child-care centers, churches— and the list goes on. Look around. What do you have to share? A "spirit of generosity" means open-handedly giving time, energy, and creativity, as well as monetary resources. Great is the reward of the person who generously gives whatever he or she has to help others.

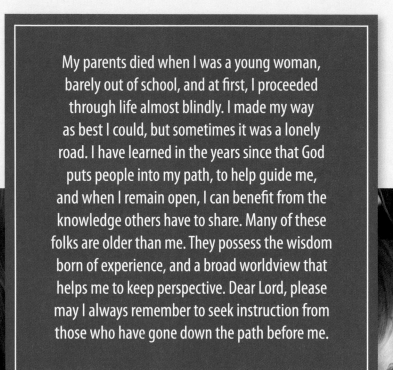

My parents died when I was a young woman, barely out of school, and at first, I proceeded through life almost blindly. I made my way as best I could, but sometimes it was a lonely road. I have learned in the years since that God puts people into my path, to help guide me, and when I remain open, I can benefit from the knowledge others have to share. Many of these folks are older than me. They possess the wisdom born of experience, and a broad worldview that helps me to keep perspective. Dear Lord, please may I always remember to seek instruction from those who have gone down the path before me.

$\mathcal{E}$arlier this week I took it upon myself to visit a local botanic garden. It is just minutes from my home, but I don't often think to go there. I went on a weekday this time, which meant that the park was much less crowded. I appreciated the solitude, and chose to walk a path that winds around a small lake and through pinewoods. The path is made of wood chips, and as I rounded a bend, I heard a crunching noise, as if someone else were walking and enjoying the bright day. I expected to encounter another hiker. Imagine my surprise when I instead found myself face to face with a deer! The doe looked at me with clear brown eyes, unafraid, and I tried to remain perfectly still. I do not think I exaggerate when I say that we shared a moment; then she regained herself and bounded away. I am so glad I made the effort to visit the botanic garden that day! Dear Lord, thank you for an encounter that filled my spirit. Thank you for this world.

> $\mathcal{T}$his is the day which the Lord hath made; we will rejoice and be glad in it.
> —Psalm 118:24

Everyone has power. Some power is more obvious than others, but we all have some, nonetheless. Power is the ability, capacity, and strength to do something—to do anything! It can be easy to feel overwhelmed and powerless by the magnitude of the issues that surround us, but we can all choose to be proactive instead of just sitting back and worrying and complaining. We can't solve every problem, but we can do our part. When you look around you, what bothers you most? If you are most concerned about the homeless, donate money or supplies to a local shelter or volunteer in some way. If you worry about kids dropping out of school, volunteer to be a tutor or a mentor. We all have the power to make some difference, and who knows what big changes might come out of "small" work. Our choices are our power! God, today I will summon my power and use it to achieve some good.

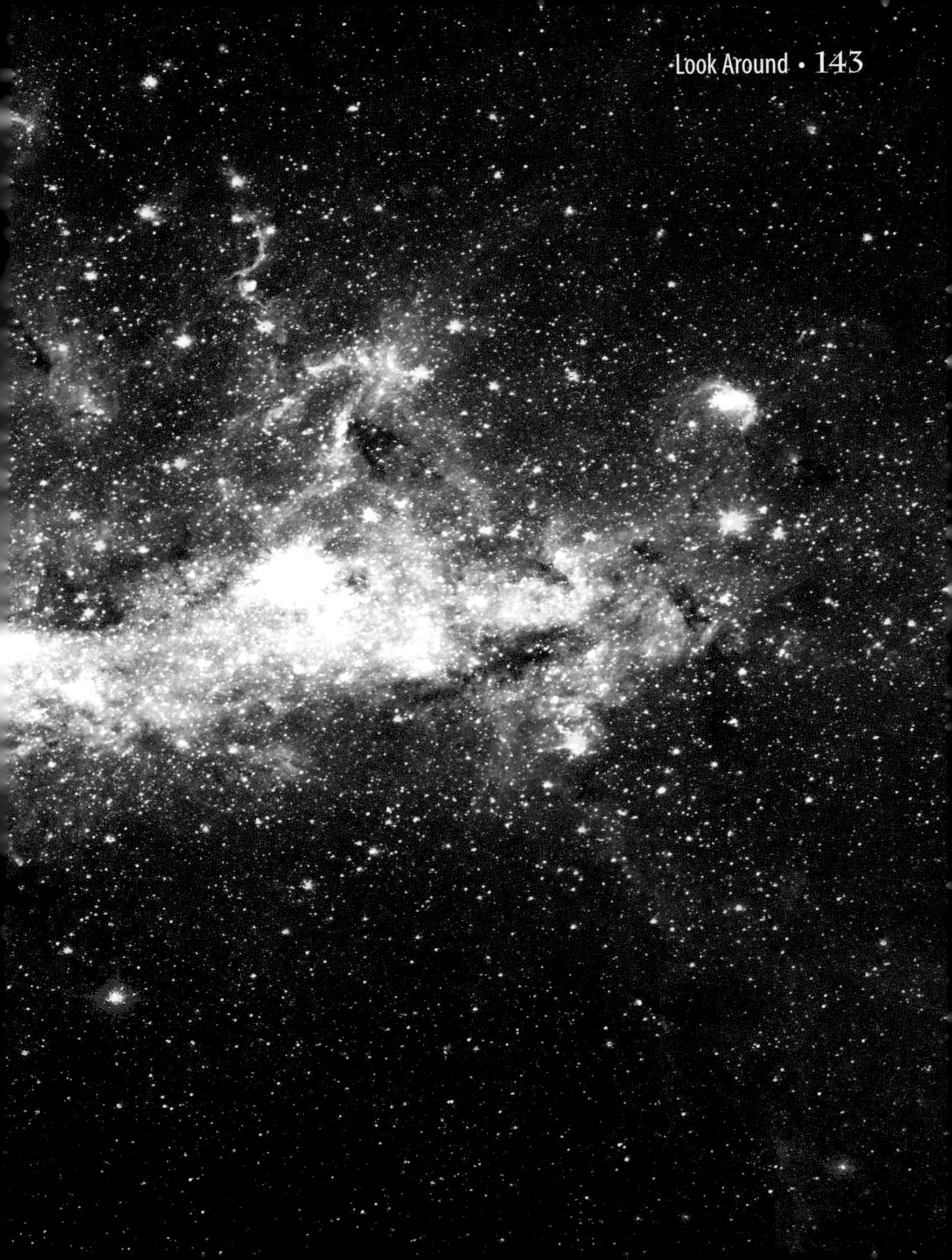

In every thing give thanks: for this is the will of God in Christ Jesus concerning you.
—1 Thessalonians 5:18

It's been a challenging year. My husband works in a volatile industry, and was laid off after his company merged with another. The layoff came as a surprise, and at a time when my we have been hit with some unexpected expenses, chiefly for home maintenance as we deal with an old roof and an older furnace. And yet, there are blessings. His company gave him a generous severance, which allows him time to figure out next steps for his career without panicking. We have savings that will help us finance the new roof, and I am reminded to be grateful that we have a roof over our heads! Ours is a happy home, filled with children and pets, books and music and sunlight. Dear Lord, even in hard times, there is always something for which I can be grateful.

*O*pposites don't attract nearly as often as they repel, if we are to believe the headlines. Pick a race, color, creed, or lifestyle, Lord of all, and we'll find something to fight about. Deliver us from stereotypes. Inspire us to spot value in everyone we meet. As we dodge the curses and hatred, we are relieved there is room for all beneath your wings.
Bless our diversity; may it flourish.

Chapter 6

SPEAK OUT

✴

Thank you, God, for the wisdom to know when to speak, what to say, and how to say it. Guard my mouth today from any form of foolishness, that in all circumstances I might honor you with my words.

But sanctify the Lord God in your hearts: and be ready always to give an answer to every man that asketh you a reason of the hope that is in you with meekness and fear.

—1 Peter 3:15

Serena and her husband Jim moved to their new home during winter, and she'd looked forward to the neighborhood's annual summer block party. She figured she'd meet new people; what she didn't anticipate was that her faith might be challenged. "So you're one of those *religious* types?" a woman laughed, upon learning that Serena and Jim attended a church nearby. Though uncomfortable, Serena dug deep: "Yes," she responded with polite firmness. "We've found happiness in our new church home." Dear Lord, sometimes I am asked to justify my faith; sometimes I am even mocked for it. Please strengthen my heart and give me the right words and spirit to articulate my belief.

$\mathcal{D}$arcy's friend Amanda, an agnostic, has always been comfortable expressing her ideas about religion. Though their viewpoints differ, Darcy has always respected Amanda's ability to speak calmly and clearly about her perspective. And engaging in dialogue with her friend has helped Darcy, who draws strength from her faith, to articulate her own ideas. "It's funny, but I learned, from Amanda, to be unafraid of expressing what I believe," she said. "Having to explain my faith has even strengthened it." God, may I never be embarrassed by my faith or feel shy about explaining what I believe. Speaking my belief strengthens that belief.

$\mathcal{T}$hat if thou shalt confess with thy mouth the Lord Jesus, and shalt believe in thine heart that God hath raised him from the dead, thou shalt be saved.
—Romans 10:9

$\mathcal{W}$hen my college roommate started acting erratically, having episodes of mania in which she talked fast, spent money wildly, and needed little sleep, followed by bouts of depression where it was tough to motivate her to get out of bed and go class, the signs were familiar. These are the signs my sister and uncle exhibited before they were diagnosed with bipolar disorder and sought treatment. But I know that a family history of mental illness doesn't make me a psychiatrist. I want to speak up about my concerns without risking our friendship. Lord, please help me find the right words that will help this situation.

*A*ll scripture is given by inspiration
of God, and is profitable for doctrine,
for reproof, for correction, for instruction
in righteousness.
—2 Timothy 3:16

Carla does not consider herself the type of person who
proselytizes; she believes actions speak louder than words.
But she personally finds the scriptures to be beautiful,
particularly the book of Psalms. She's committed some
passages to memory, and will sometimes quote them as a
way of sharing their beauty. "I guess this is how I express
my faith," Carla said. "To me, it's like sharing a poem.
I'm communicating something that brings me joy."
Dear Lord, please help me to be a teacher in my own way!

Speaking to yourselves in psalms and hymns and spiritual songs, singing and making melody in your heart to the Lord.
—Ephesians 5:19

*T*hough Marilyn loves to sing, she sometimes can't stay in tune. When she was a child, her choir instructor would often tell her to "just mouth the words." Marilyn became shy about her voice; it wasn't until years later, when her boyfriend Erik came upon her singing hymns in the kitchen, that she was encouraged to express herself again in song. "Singing makes me happy," Marilyn says. "Erik reminded me that God doesn't care if I'm note perfect!" Dear Lord, you embolden us to speak out in many ways, one of which is the gift of song. May I never fear that my song is not sweet enough!

When Ruth's friend Nora encouraged her to join in a neighborhood effort to go door to door and collect canned goods for the homeless, Ruth was at first hesitant; her natural shyness seemed to preclude such activity. But after praying and reflecting on her fears, she decided to move outside her comfort zone and help out. The experience was uplifting: it felt good to be acting—and speaking—on behalf of those in need. Lord, please embolden me to speak out for those less fortunate than myself.

Open thy mouth, judge righteously,
and plead the cause of
the poor and needy.
—Proverbs 31:9

Casting down imaginations, and every high thing that exalteth itself against the knowledge of God, and bringing into captivity every thought to the obedience of Christ.

—2 Corinthians 10:5

Beth, an attorney, is invited to constantly debate on behalf of what she believes is right. Every day she goes in to work, she deals with conflict, and her "opponents" are articulate people with well-crafted arguments. It can be draining and emotionally taxing, but she is inspired by God's exhortation to speak out. Dear Lord, Corinthians tells me that you were there for people in biblical times when they had to debate. I believe that you are there for me, too, every day, when I am challenged to speak out.

I have had dinner nearly every Wednesday with my friend Katie for years now. They were often the highlight of my week and therapeutic for me, as I can tell Katie anything. When Katie started dating a new guy, she sort of fell off the map. Our dinners have gone from weekly events to monthly and even less frequent now. I want to give her space and be supportive of her new relationship, but I miss my friend. Lord, help me speak up about my feelings and preserve our friendship.

*H*ave you ever been in a situation where a leader was asked a question he or she obviously didn't want to be asked? Maybe it challenged them, or took the discussion in a different direction than what they wanted. Or maybe they just didn't know the answer! In any case, a question, even a difficult or unwelcome one, is rarely actually inappropriate. Perhaps it misses the point, but in that case, it is merely a misunderstanding that can quickly be cleared up. Questions just promote discussion, and discussion is merely communication—that's how things get done! Lord, today I will not hesitate to ask a question, and if a question is asked of me, I will think carefully and answer it as best I can.

After a routine dental procedure went awry, Megan became very ill. She contracted blood poisoning and the pain in her jaw was beyond anything she'd ever experienced. Thanks to antibiotics and sound medical care, Megan recovered, but now, even months later, when she wakes pain-free she still gives thanks to God. "It took an extreme situation to remind me of the importance of thanking God; being grateful inspires joy, and I feel closer to God than ever," Megan says. Dear Lord, I understand how important it is to give thanks to you. It draws me closer to you, and is good for my heart.

By him therefore let us offer the sacrifice of praise to God continually, that is, the fruit of our lips giving thanks to his name.

—Hebrews 13:15

*M*any of us have had the experience in which a seemingly casual question has led to a deep, meaningful discussion. In these moments we feel alive and productive and sense a deep kinship with others. Discuss! Communicate! It is how most things get done. Heavenly Father, today I will be open to communication with those around me. I will voice my opinion and be respectful of the opinions of others.

Selma's sister Heather had always enjoyed a glass or two of wine over dinner, but increasingly, Selma noticed that Heather was drinking in excess. Selma doesn't like confrontation, but things came to a head after an unpleasant, alcohol-fueled incident at a family dinner. With love and some trepidation, Selma sat down with Heather and encouraged her to seek treatment. It was a difficult, but necessary, conversation. Though tears were shed, Heather agreed to get help. Dear Lord, speaking the truth publicly is not always easy to do, but it is important. It is an act of love. Please help me to do so with strength and grace.

But speaking the truth in love, may grow up into him in all things, which is the head, even Christ.

—Ephesians 4:15

Is any among you afflicted?
let him pray.
Is any merry?
let him sing psalms.
—James 5:13

Denise's mother Jenny always tried to include God in her daily life. When Jenny faced challenges, she prayed. When she experienced joy, she sang hymns. Now that Denise is a mother herself, she tries to model this same way of being. "By speaking up and reaching out to God in good times as well as bad, I feel more connected spiritually," Denise says. "My mom gave me that gift, and I hope to pass it on to my son." Dear God, connecting with you is a form of speaking up; may I always remember this!

*W*hen sixteen-year-old Kate auditioned for the school play, she was surprised to be cast in a substantial role. She loved rehearsals and connected with fellow cast members, but as the date of the show approached, she found herself increasingly consumed with doubt. What if she froze on stage? She wished she could drop out of the play, but her dad encouraged her to pray for courage. She did so. "I'm so glad I stuck with it," Kate says now. God, I know it's okay to have stage fright, but I mustn't let fear stop me. Thank you for helping me work through my fears.

*T*hen spake the Lord to Paul in the night by a vision, Be not afraid, but speak, and hold not thy peace.

—Acts 18:9

> *And* they which went before rebuked him,
> that he should hold his peace: but he cried so much
> the more, Thou son of David, have mercy on me.
>
> —Luke 18:39

The college track was not fruitful or satisfying for Carole, but when she told friends she was thinking of leaving school to start her own business cutting hair, they discouraged her. "I let myself be convinced that it was foolish to stray from a certain path," Carole says now. It took another difficult school year for her to decide she was ready to strike out on her own. Now she's not only successful in her business, but personally fulfilled. God, Luke's story of the blind man fills me with hope. Thank you for reminding me that I mustn't let others tell me "what I can't do."

I wish to extend my love, Lord. So give me hands quick to work on behalf of the weak. Cause my feet to move swiftly in aid of the needy. Let my mouth speak words of encouragement and new life. And give my heart an ever-deepening joy through it all.

$\mathcal{L}$ord, sometimes when I speak to others about my faith, I see
doubt in their faces. Faith in you doesn't always appeal to the
"rational" adult in us, unfortunately. Please give us the grace that
will enable us to come to you with open minds, open hearts—
and open arms. I know that once we clear our minds of all that
we think we know, all will become clear to us through you.

Lynne's six-year-old daughter Phoebe has a severe peanut allergy, but the school Phoebe attends did not have any protocols in place should the girl experience an allergic reaction. At first, the school administration did not appreciate the severity of Phoebe's allergy, which is in fact life threatening. Lynne's initial efforts to bring attention to her daughter's condition were treated dismissively; she had to dig deep to be the firm, wise advocate her daughter's situation demanded. Dear Lord, please help me to be ready to speak up for those who cannot speak for themselves. May I be a wise and thoughtful advocate.

Open thy mouth for the dumb in the cause of all such as are appointed to destruction.
—Proverbs 31:8

One of my oldest friends, Beth, recently and unexpectedly lost her husband. Dan was killed in a freak car accident, and Beth and her children have been blindsided by the loss. I have spent a lot of time with the family since the accident, and see how even the most well-meaning people have sometimes said hurtful things to Beth in their efforts to show concern. I want to avoid causing my friend any more pain, and so for the most part have tried to provide solace with my quiet presence. But I know that the right words can assuage grief. Dear Lord, grant me the wisdom to comfort my friends in their time of need. Help me to know what to say.

But I would strengthen you with my mouth, and the moving of my lips should assuage your grief.
—Job 16:5

We never know what's going on in the life of another person. The guy who cuts me off in traffic or the checkout clerk who reacts to a query with impatience. The way someone reacts doesn't always reflect how they feel about me; it is often instead a response to the complex circumstances of their life on that given day. God, help me remember to respond to others with grace and kindness—to put good out into the world just for the sake of doing so—for the right words spoken to someone at the right time might lift the worry that burdens another's heart.

Heaviness in the heart of man maketh it stoop: but a good word maketh it glad.
—Proverbs 12:25

*L*ord, I have the conviction that your presence in my life makes it better: when I let you into my heart, you inform the way I treat others, the way I approach work, the way I move through my days. And good things are meant to be shared! God, help me to share with others the good wisdom I have learned from you. I don't have to proselytize. That's not my style. But through my actions I can demonstrate my beliefs, and in this way create a ripple effect: good begetting good begetting good, with results far beyond what I might even be able to apprehend.

> *A*nd the things that thou hast heard
> of me among many witnesses,
> the same commit thou to faithful men,
> who shall be able to teach others also.
> —2 Timothy 2:2

*L*ord, in a society that condones deception and half-truths, I long to teach my children the importance of honesty, of keeping promises, and of doing what they say they will do. Help me to begin with myself. Keep me always aware of my own integrity in my relationships with others. Let me be a person my family and friends can count on to speak truthfully and to deliver what is promised.

When I'm waiting through the turmoil of doing the right thing at the cost of my personal comfort, Lord, help me to be patient. Help me not to sabotage your works by trying to fix things in my own way. Oh, it's not always easy to hold my tongue, but if I wait until you open the door for me to speak—and I look to you for the right attitude when I do talk—then I won't have to deal with all the regrets and what-ifs. Grant me a patient spirit, Father.

Speak, move, act in peace, as if you were in prayer. In truth, this is prayer.

—Francois de Salignace de La Mothe Fenelon

*A*nd when we cried unto the Lord, he heard
our voice, and sent an angel, and hath brought
us forth out of Egypt.

—Numbers 20:16

*M*y friend and I have had a falling out, Lord. The atmosphere is strained between us; the air is chilly. I don't know
what I've said or done to cause this breach in our relationship.
I only know we're both at odds. Relieve the anguish that I feel,
Lord. Show me how to break the silence. Help me take the first
step to mend this rift between us, then you can do the rest.
Heal us with your love.

$\mathcal{L}$ord, my temper can run short. Everywhere I go I have to stand in line; I feel rushed and stressed, and it's easy to get caught up in the frenetic pace. Teach me to use time in line as time to pray, and let us speak and interact with others in a courteous fashion.

Chapter 7

KEEP MOVING

*Having faith in God is important,
but even he expects us to move our feet.
Without taking action, his words of wisdom go unheeded,
and his will goes unfulfilled. We best serve ourselves
when we listen for his word, then move forward boldly.*

Jesus said unto her, I am the
resurrection, and the life:
he that believeth in me,
though he were dead,
yet shall he live.

—John 11:25

When the going gets tough, women keep going. We cannot stop the flow of life when we feel weak or tired. We must carry on and keep moving, no matter how slow or small our progress.

$\mathcal{I}$t is funny to look back at certain accomplishments. It is such a relief to have them done. In hindsight things seem so clear, but while you're in the midst of your work, the end can sometimes seem so far in the distance; it can be easy to get discouraged. Once we've achieved our goal we can look back at our unknowing selves and say, "I can't believe I almost gave up at that point, when I was so close!"
Keep going—you are getting there!

**Lord, today I will keep going no matter what.
I will not give in to discouragement.**

$\mathcal{D}$ear God, when obstacles threaten to derail me from the path towards my goals, give me the strength to go forward anyway, even if it means taking a little detour. Help me keep my pace, and not become weak of body or spirit over the long road ahead.

Therefore I say unto you, what things soever ye desire, when ye pray, believe that ye receive them, and ye shall have them.
—Mark 11:24

God, the knowledge that your promises will be fulfilled keeps me going through the toughest of days and nights. I know if I stay strong and power through, I will be richly rewarded in body, mind, and spirit.

$\mathscr{A}$ s a parent, what I wish for my daughter Anne is an easy path. When she struggles with her studies or experiences conflicts with friends, my heart aches. I know, however, that no one can be shielded from pain indefinitely, and that it is adversity as well as our joys that shape us. My grandfather used to say that misfortune can build character, and I see that in my daughter. Challenges have shown her that she possesses an inner steel, even as they've demanded she develop patience and compassion. Dear Lord, help me to guide Anne so that she might meet hardship with strength, patience, and grace. May adversity help her to grow as a person.

> $\mathscr{A}$ nd not only so, but we glory in tribulations also: knowing that tribulation worketh patience.
> —Romans 5:3

When I walk with God, I become stronger and wiser each day. No obstacle can delay me. No challenge can destroy me. When I move in God's will, no difficulty can defeat me. When I heed God's word, no goal can elude me!

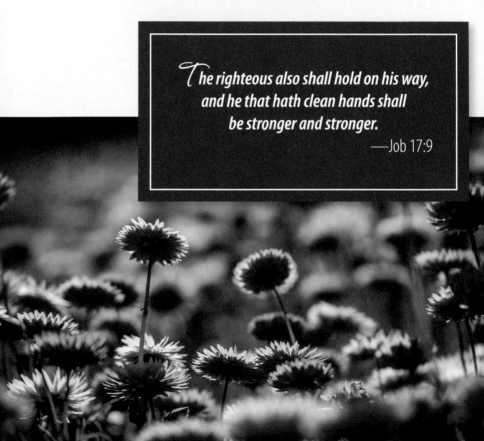

The righteous also shall hold on his way, and he that hath clean hands shall be stronger and stronger.

—Job 17:9

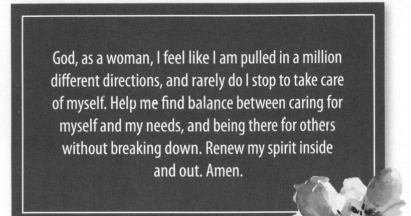

God, as a woman, I feel like I am pulled in a million different directions, and rarely do I stop to take care of myself. Help me find balance between caring for myself and my needs, and being there for others without breaking down. Renew my spirit inside and out. Amen.

God Almighty, hear my prayer. Give me wings to soar when my feet get tired. Give me manna from heaven when my stomach growls with hunger. Give me fuel for my spirit when my mood is low. God, hear my prayer!

Now faith is the substance of things hoped for, the evidence of things not seen.
—Hebrews 11:1

Dear Lord, I am feeling more hopeful these days. For a while, I forgot to include your loving guidance in my life. I forgot that if I pray and meditate and just get silent enough to listen, you always give me the answers I seek, and the direction I need to overcome anything. I pray for continued guidance and wisdom, and that I may always live from a place of hope instead of fear, and a place of possibilities instead of limitations. You are my wings and my rock, allowing me to both soar higher and stay grounded. No matter what I may be facing, your presence gives me the hope I need to keep moving forward with my head held high and my heart strong and fearless.

God created women as powerful, loving beings.
But as women, we get tired and worn out.
We burn the candle at both ends.
The only way to keep moving forward is to make
sure we are healthy, strong, and at peace,
so we can then help others.

The great thing in this world is not so much where we stand, as in what direction we are moving: To reach the port of heaven, we must sail sometimes with the wind and sometimes against it,—but we must sail, and not drift, nor lie at anchor.

—Oliver Wendell Holmes

When all seems lost and you want to stop, remember God made you to shine and be epic! Small hearts give up, but you have the heart of a lion. Know that with God all things are possible. Keep on keepin' on and let the lion within you roar!

L ord God, my feet are as sore as my spirit is exhausted. Help me carry on and do the things I must each day for my family, my community, and myself. Teach me to walk even when it hurts and share the gifts you have given me with the world.

Whenever you take a journey—whether across town to a familiar home or across the country to a new place—remember to take God with you. God will guide your path, watch your steps, and keep you company all along the way.

$\mathcal{I}$ recently graduated from college, and while I look for a job in my field of study, which is geology, I've been working a series of lower-paying jobs to pay the bills. I have managed to create a life I'm proud of. I pride myself on being independent and not living beyond my means. But my student loan debt is substantial, and the old car I've been driving since high school doesn't have many more miles left. My current jobs do not offer health insurance. Some days I feel discouraged that I have not yet found the work for which my education has prepared me. Some nights I can't sleep for worrying about finances, or what expenses lie around the corner. God, help me to remember that you are there: to support me, and imbue me with strength and wisdom. Help me to remember that you will provide.

> $\mathcal{T}$herefore I say unto you, Take no thought for your life, what ye shall eat, or what ye shall drink; nor yet for your body, what ye shall put on. Is not the life more than meat, and the body than raiment?
>
> —Matthew 6:25

*P*lease forgive me when I complain, Lord. I don't mean to ignore the things that are good in my life—and there are many. It's just that pain and struggle and weariness shout so loudly that sometimes they're all I can hear. When I need to cry a little, let me cry on your shoulder where I know I'll be heard and understood, consoled and encouraged. Other people might minimize what I'm going through or rant about things I can't control. Neither is helpful in moving me toward a better place. But when I pour out my discouragement to you, I know that you'll listen and then gently turn my heart back toward what brings strength and grace to carry on. You even make me able to give thanks and rejoice in you. Thank you for being there, for listening, and for lifting me up.

O God, grief is taking me somewhere new. Feeling your guiding hand, I will hold on and keep moving. Amen.

How do I say goodbye to someone I've loved so much in this life, Father? To let them go, to live life with that empty spot where they once were feels so awkward and unnatural. It seems wrong to carry on without them. Something inside me shouts, "As if I could!" And yet I must, and I do, and it's so difficult. How do I find "normal" now in those places where we always stood together? Please help me. I don't know how. Carry me, keep my tears as a memorial, and grant me that quiet healing that happens as grief takes its course. And please, even in this grief, let me find joy in the memories of our time together on this earth.

Now therefore ye are no more strangers and foreigners, but fellowcitizens with the saints, and of the household of God.

—Ephesians 2:19

Community enriches us, granting us a sense of belonging, mutual support, and opportunities to exchange ideas and knowledge. But in today's transient culture, people move all the time, often because of job opportunities or changes. A move to a new place can be an exciting opportunity, of course. But uprooting from a familiar place, with its reassuring ties, can be unsettling. You had found someone who cut your hair just right; you knew whom to call when the pipe under the sink sprouted a leak. Perhaps most importantly, you had a network of friends and loved ones who helped you feel at home in the world. It takes time to reestablish a sense of community after a move, but God is present to help us on the journey. In an unfamiliar place, have faith that you will find your people.

$\mathcal{M}$ ost things we desire take perseverance, don't they? When groups of citizens in a young country banded together to resist laws they believed were unfair, they persevered and won their freedom as a prize. Years later different groups of people banded together to end slavery, and again, freedom was gained through perseverance. What if those people had not persevered? It would have been easy to just quit, but we are thankful for their perseverance. Today, if a job or task tires or deflates me, I will not give in until it is finished. I will persevere, and I will be proud of myself afterward.

$\mathcal{P}$ erseverance will accomplish all things.

—American Proverb

*Be strong and of a good courage;
be not afraid, neither be thou dismayed:
for the Lord thy God is with thee
whithersoever thou goest.*

—Joshua 1:9

Thank you, Lord, for never being missing in action. You're with me all the time, everywhere, without fail. Please keep this knowledge in the forefront of my mind today so I'll be encouraged and emboldened to move through each challenge without feeling intimidated, fearful, or ashamed. May I always be kept safe because of your keeping power at work in my life. In your name, I pray.

*T*he struggles we face on our life journeys give us that fine patina that we can eventually claim as wisdom. Having grown up in a happy, nearly perfect family, it never occurred to me that I might end up struggling financially to raise four children on my own. Never dreamed it, but once it was my reality, I embraced it and grew from the struggles it entailed. With those struggles came confidence and greater empathy for others.

Today I will face each struggle with confidence and determination.

I have learned that success is to be measured not so much by the position that one has reached in life as by the obstacles which he has overcome while trying to succeed.
—Booker T. Washington

*D*ear God, hear my prayer. I am suffering and in need of your merciful blessings. Please take me into your arms. Give me the courage to keep going through difficult times and the fortitude to move beyond the outer illusions of pain and despair. Only you can heal me, God. In praise and thanks, amen.

Faith is a true sign of bravery. It is looking forward to the future despite challenges and adversity; it is trusting in something that you can neither see nor touch yet knowing it is always there guiding you along life's path.

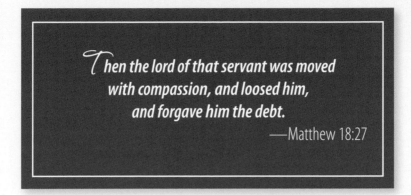

Then the lord of that servant was moved with compassion, and loosed him, and forgave him the debt.

—Matthew 18:27

God, I aspire to be the person you want me to be, to live the life you want for me, but sometimes I struggle. I have a friend to whom I lent money; it has become apparent that not only will she not be able to repay what she owes, but she has also been avoiding me. I caught sight of her in town yesterday, and she literally crossed the street to avoid any interaction. Even when I called out to her, she would not meet my eye. I know she is ashamed that she cannot repay me, but I'm disappointed in her. I wish I'd never lent her the money.

**Please grant me the compassion and grace to
forgive this debt, and move on.**

Chapter 8

LIFT OTHERS

*ive me eyes, O God, to take a second look at those
who think, act, and look different from me.
Help me take seriously your image of them.
Equip me with acceptance and courage as I hold
out a welcoming hand, knowing that you
are where strangers' hands meet.*

And Moses called unto Joshua,
and said unto him in the sight of all Israel,
Be strong and of a good courage: for thou
must go with this people unto the land
which the Lord hath sworn unto their
fathers to give them; and thou shalt
cause them to inherit it.

—Deuteronomy 31:7

Danielle's mother Olivia had always been the matriarch, the "glue" that held her family together. When Olivia was diagnosed with Parkinson's disease, Danielle, as the eldest of her siblings, knew she needed to step up and be strong for everyone. "I suddenly was called upon to mediate and make decisions that affected the entire family," Danielle remembers. "It was ultimately a time of growth, but I felt challenged. I prayed for guidance a lot." Dear God, please embolden me to be a leader, just as Moses uplifted Joshua to lead the Israelites into the promised land.

In a church or family, praising can have the nice effect of building up others and spreading cheer. In our house, we'll occasionally indulge in what we call "love bombardment": someone will get singled out for a blitz of praise, during which everyone else in the house heaps compliments upon the designated recipient. We usually focus on someone who's had a long or challenging day. It doesn't take long for everyone to be caught up in laughter, and the object of affection gets a nice boost. Everyone needs a lift sometimes, and taking part in praise bombardment has proven, in our house at least, to be a balm for all concerned.

Dear Lord, help me to remember that attitudes are infectious.

*W*ho, when he came, and had seen the grace of God, was glad, and exhorted them all, that with purpose of heart they would cleave unto the Lord.

—Acts 11:23

When layoffs hit the company where Christine works, morale fell. "I manage a small staff," Christine explains. "It was up to me to uplift my direct reports during a time when none of us were sure that we'd still have a job when we came to work each morning. I firmly believe God helped me through that chapter." Things have improved for Christine's employer, but she learned something from the experience: "With God's help, I can inspire others." Dear Lord, in Acts we learn about Barnabas, who encouraged early Christians to strengthen their faith even as they were persecuted. Help me to remember that one person can make a difference!

*L*ittle things can mean a lot. Emma's mom Diane had had a hard day at work: Emma saw it on her mom's face the moment Diane came through the door. Without prompting, Emma made dinner; she even threw together an impromptu dessert, cooked in a mug in the microwave and, crucially, involving chocolate. "I was so discouraged when I got home," Diane remembers. "But my evening was, truly, transformed by loving-kindness."

Lord, you want us to uplift the weak and exhausted.
May I provide support to those who are worn down in life.

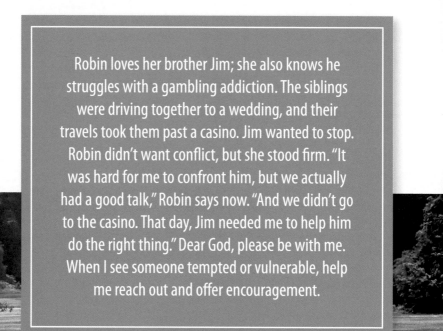

Robin loves her brother Jim; she also knows he struggles with a gambling addiction. The siblings were driving together to a wedding, and their travels took them past a casino. Jim wanted to stop. Robin didn't want conflict, but she stood firm. "It was hard for me to confront him, but we actually had a good talk," Robin says now. "And we didn't go to the casino. That day, Jim needed me to help him do the right thing." Dear God, please be with me. When I see someone tempted or vulnerable, help me reach out and offer encouragement.

And nd all they that were about them strengthened their hands with vessels of silver, with gold, with goods, and with beasts, and with precious things, beside all that was willingly offered.

—Ezra 1:6

*S*chool has always been hard for eight-year-old Gina, who struggles academically but also, sometimes, with social cues. Gina has a tutor to help her with the academics, but Gina's mom Sue also knows that little tokens—glittery pencils, a small stuffed toy to fit in a pocket—help encourage her daughter. "I wish school was easier for Gina," Sue says. "But I know there are things I can do to help her navigate her day."

Dear God, gifts are excellent tokens that encourage and uplift people. May I remember that such a gesture can do much good.

> $\mathcal{S}$o the carpenter encouraged the goldsmith, and he that smootheth with the hammer him that smote the anvil, saying, It is ready for the sodering: and he fastened it with nails, that it should not be moved.
>
> —Isaiah 41:7

$\mathcal{V}$anessa's coworker Greg went above and beyond on a challenging project, and she told him so. Only later did she understand how much her warm words meant: "It turns out Greg was in the process of filing for divorce; he was under a lot of stress, and feeling a little lost personally," Vanessa remembers. "He told me later that my praise meant a lot during a difficult chapter."

Dear Lord, I do not always appreciate what a sincere compliment might mean to someone who needs it. Help me to remember to uplift others at work.

In an age of all things digital, Tamara still writes letters to send by post. She writes to her brother. She writes to a favorite aunt. "Sure, I use e-mail, too," she shares. "And I text. But I know I'm always thrilled when I get a 'real' letter in my mailbox, rather than just bills and junk mail. There is permanence to a written note, on lovely paper, that gives me a lift. I hope my letters bring the same kind of joy."

**Dear Lord, written words have lasting power.
May what I write bring solace and joy!**

*Which when they had read,
they rejoiced for the consolation.*
—Acts 15:31

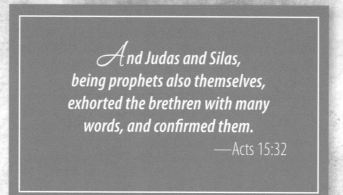

And Judas and Silas,
being prophets also themselves,
exhorted the brethren with many
words, and confirmed them.
—Acts 15:32

*M*argie has lived long, and seen much; life has not always been kind to her. But experience has made Margie wise, not bitter, and she has the gift of imparting that wisdom in a gentle, offhand way. "I learned from her and I didn't even know I was learning!" Margie's granddaughter Alice says, adding, "This was especially important when I was a teen, and didn't think anyone had *anything* to teach me! Grandma's lessons are delivered with tremendous grace."

Lord, teaching others can uplift! Help me to share with others what I know; help me to be a strong, wise teacher.

*E*very day most of us come into contact with someone who is suffering, and it usually gives us an empty feeling in the middle of our being. Helping others helps them, of course, but it also helps us. We get a feeling of accomplishment and a sense of community. We know that at times we have been and will again be the recipient of others' help, whether in the form of a lead on a job, a visit when we were grieving, or a helping hand when we were on a tight deadline. Community works best when this give and take is in smooth, constant motion.

**Heavenly Father, today I will be ready to give if called upon, and I will also be ready to take if I am in need.
I will be an active participant in my community.**

*S*haron has been participating in a morning exercise class for three years; the class gets her day off to a good start. A few weeks ago she was surprised when a classmate, a woman she hardly knows, approached her after the morning session and thanked her for always maintaining an attitude of positivity. "She said my cheerfulness uplifts her," Sharon remembers. "I was gratified—and humbled to realize that how I act can affect even those I barely know." You never know whom you might inspire through your actions. Dear God, may I live a life of faith, cheer, and humility; help me to live in a way that uplifts others.

*T*hat is, that I may be comforted together with you by the mutual faith both of you and me.

—Romans 1:12

> *With good will doing service, as to the Lord, and not to men.*
>
> —Ephesians 6:7

When Jessica's friend Misty was struggling through a divorce, Jessica tried to be present for her friend, offering babysitting, hot meals, and a listening ear. Misty, consumed with anxiety about her future, was not always appreciative of the sacrifices Jessica made to support her. "It was a tough year," Jessica remembers now. "Our friendship has regained its balance, but there were times I prayed for guidance because I felt Misty was taking my efforts for granted." Dear God, my efforts to uplift others are not always reciprocated—or even appreciated. May I do the right thing for you, not for gratitude or anything I might receive in return.

*D*ear Lord, generosity is your way, and I seek to emulate your goodness when I give of my time, energy, and resources. It feels good to give of myself—giving draws upon my best self—and when I do so, please be with me. Remind me not to become puffed up in pride about my acts of generosity; remind me not to call attention to what I have done. I give for you, and to lift others up, not to make myself look good.

*A*s we extend our hands and hearts toward others in love, something wonderful happens: Our own spirits become healed, our natures more refined, and our souls stronger. We become happier and more at peace. Try starting a new "exercise" program of loving kindness and service, and see how much good you can do for your own heart in the process. Father, today I will be the one who reaches out to lift and help another.

I once heard a story about a farmer whose fruit won awards at the State Fair year after year. He had guarded his secret closely, letting others speculate on whether it was in the soil, special additives, or expensive seeds. One year he decided to finally reveal the secret to his prize-winning crops. "I've been giving my seeds away for years," he said. The farmer explained how his crops couldn't grow so well in isolation; they had to be cross-pollinated. Therefore the better his neighbors' seeds were, the better their crops were, and then the better his crops were too. This lesson can apply to human communities as well. It is in our best interests for our neighbors to thrive, as it lifts up our whole community. When we look out for and support each other, we all benefit. Today, God, I will engage in an activity that will benefit my community and me. Perhaps I will sign up to volunteer at my local school, library, or museum.

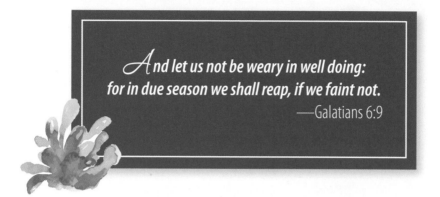

And let us not be weary in well doing: for in due season we shall reap, if we faint not.
—Galatians 6:9

*N*ancy's brother Ed has suffered from depression for years. He's on medication now, which helps. And Nancy tries to uplift him (and sometimes succeeds) with daily texts, movie nights together, and the occasional dinner out. "Ed's depression has been a learning experience for me," Nancy shares. "I can be there for him, I can't stop trying, but I cannot expect that every one of my efforts will make a difference. I have to be at peace with that." Lord, I am discouraged because my efforts to uplift others seem to mean little. Help me to not lose heart. Help me to keep trying.

Though Tracy's mom is wheelchair-bound, she's still game for adventure. And Tracy, at 60, is grateful she still has the strength to take her mom out. "It can be a big production," Tracy says. "It'll be snowing, and getting my mom in and out of the car with the chair can be tiring. But I'm glad I can still do it: we go out for coffee at our favorite diner, or we'll go shopping together. It's always worth it!"

God, sometimes uplifting others means offering actual physical help. Please grant me the literal strength to be able to do so!

But Moses hands were heavy; and they took a stone, and put it under him, and he sat thereon; and Aaron and Hur stayed up his hands, the one on the one side, and the other on the other side; and his hands were steady until the going down of the sun.

—Exodus 17:12

Judge not, and ye shall not be judged: condemn not, and ye shall not be condemned: forgive, and ye shall be forgiven. Give, and it shall be given unto you; good measure, pressed down, and shaken together, and running over, shall men give into your bosom. For with the same measure that ye mete withal it shall be measured to you again.

—Luke 6:37–38

We all have something to offer: time, money, expertise. God exhorts us to give generously; in his infinite wisdom, he understands that when we give, we're not just helping others (worthy in and of itself), but we also help ourselves. Studies have shown that generosity helps to manage personal stress, and have linked unselfishness and giving with a general sense of life satisfaction and a lower risk of early death. When we reach outside ourselves, we connect with others. God wants that connection, that sense of purpose and happiness, for each of us. Dear Lord, help us to connect with our best selves; help us to be generous givers.

We live in an information society. Daily, we are bombarded with news. Our phones, televisions, computers, and tablets keep us breathlessly apprised of the latest events. It is good to be informed, and technology is a gift. But an adverse effect of all-information-all-the-time is a sort of numbing of the senses. "Another earthquake?" we shrug. "Another tragedy?" It can be an effort to dig deep and access caring, and yet compassion is a godly virtue. God wants us to experience concern for the sufferings of others. Dear Lord, help us to strike a balance in our information intake so that we retain compassion for those in need. May we never become callous to others' misfortune.

Thus speaketh the Lord of hosts, saying, Execute true judgment, and shew mercy and compassions every man to his brother.
—Zechariah 7:9

*I*f we are strong, we have a responsibility to use that gift to lift those around us rather than pushing them further down to make us feel better about ourselves. Besides, when anyone succeeds, it usually lifts everyone around them a little bit too.

Today, Lord, I will make an effort to help those who have less than I do.

> $\mathcal{S}$he stretcheth out her hand to the poor;
> yea, she reacheth forth her hands to the needy.
> —Proverbs 31:20

$\mathcal{M}$y husband and I work hard, but some months money is tight. Although we will never be what our culture considers wealthy, I am grateful that we have what we need. I read recently about the devastating flooding in Texas, and was reminded of how generosity can manifest itself in different ways. While we can donate a small amount of cash, I also, perhaps more crucially, can devote some of my time to volunteer efforts. I am healthy and can even donate blood. God, I am blessed in so many ways; please help me to remember the importance of generosity, and how it can take many forms.

As every man hath received the gift, even so minister the same one to another, as good stewards of the manifold grace of God.

—1 Peter 4:10

It is easier to help others when my own life is going well. During those chapters in life when things are more or less on an even keel, I am filled with cheer, and I go out into the world wanting to share that goodwill. The act of service comes less easily to me when life presents challenges. When burdened by stress at work, say, or the struggles my son periodically faces from bullies at school, my tendency is to look inward. God, teach me to strive to help others no matter what is going on in my life. You serve us regardless of externals. Service is a gift from you! Remembering this puts me in the right frame of mind to serve others.

I am grateful to live in a democratic society where I can live freely and do as I please. I have a steady job, which consequently allows me to pursue multiple interests that include travel and food. I thoroughly enjoy exploring new cuisines, for example, and cooking for and eating out with friends. I feel lucky to be free to engage in such rewarding experiences—they "fill me up"—yet I also know that reaching out to others is an important part of becoming a fulfilled, evolved person. To that end, I recently signed up to volunteer with Meals on Wheels. I have already met some cool seniors, folks I likely would never have encountered in my usual orbit. I find myself looking forward to my interactions with them each week. God, help me to honor the freedom I enjoy by helping others, not just by indulging myself.

For, brethren, ye have been called unto liberty; only use not liberty for an occasion to the flesh, but by love serve one another. For all the law is fulfilled in one word, even in this; Thou shalt love thy neighbour as thyself.
—Galatians 5:13–14

One of the principle rules of religion is to lose no occasion of serving God. And since he is invisible to our eyes, we are to serve him in our neighbor, which he receives as if done to himself in person, standing visibly before us.

—John Wesley

*E*ternal God, it's so hard for us to know what to do for friends who are suffering with terminal illness or a disability. We want to be able to pour our own health and vitality into them in order to give them relief, but all we can do is care and pray for them. Use us in those situations, God. Especially when their illness lingers, encourage us to be constant encouragers to those who need regular injections of your love and concern. We trust you will heal, whether on Earth or in heaven. And we take great comfort in that.

> *B*ut the God of all grace, who hath called us unto his eternal glory by Christ Jesus, after that ye have suffered a while, make you perfect, stablish, strengthen, settle you.
>
> —1 Peter 5:10

Offering hope to others through a loving word, a thoughtful act, or a simple smile is the surest way to lift your own spirit.

It is easy to get so caught up in our own goals that we forget that our loved ones have their own goals as well. Being generous with our loved ones helps them, and it helps us grow too. By taking the focus off ourselves from time to time, we learn and experience new things that give us an expanded insight on life.

God, I will seize an opportunity to cheer someone else on today.

I wish to be of service, Lord. So give me courage to put my own hope and despair, my own doubt and fear, at the disposal of others. For how could I ever help without first being, simply . . . real?

> *I* have shewed you all things, how that so labouring ye ought to support the weak, and to remember the words of the Lord Jesus, how he said, It is more blessed to give than to receive.
>
> —Acts 20:35

I am grateful for the blessings in my life: a strong marriage, good health, and a steady job. I firmly believe that these advantages put me in a position to help those less fortunate than myself. On a fundamental level, I think that's why we're here—to assist others. But some days I do grow weary of the work constant service (either service I've elected to do or that has been thrust upon me) requires. On those days, God, please help me to remember how giving fills one spiritually. Christ taught that it is better to give than to receive; please help me to remember this on the days that I struggle.

Chapter 9

MAKE PLANS

You can have those dreams you dream.
God instilled them in you so you could
express his love out into the world.
Through your skills, talent, and creativity,
God wants you to be epic!
Make plans, and then let him work
those plans through you in a miraculous way!

Being confident of this very thing, that he which hath begun a good work in you will perform it until the day of Jesus Christ.
—Philippians 1:6

*G*od, help me become a powerful loving presence in the world. Set before me directions to the path meant for me, a path that allows me to fully express your will through my words, deeds, and actions. Amen.

Guide us, dear God, to the perfect destiny you have set out for us. Help keep us on the path to right action, right choices, and right solutions to the problems we may encounter. Help deliver us from obstacles that may detour us and lead us astray. Show us the way to fulfill your divine plan.

And be not conformed to this world: but be ye transformed by the renewing of your mind, that ye may prove what is that good, and acceptable, and perfect, will of God.

—Romans 12:2

*W*ith boldness, wonder, and expectation, I greet you this morning, God of sunrise. Gratefully, I look back to all that was good yesterday and in hope, face forward, ready for today.

*G*od has a mighty vision for my life, and I plan to live up to those expectations. Through the work I do, and the love I give, I hope to fulfill God's legacy of good in the world. I refuse to stay small when God is asking me to go big.

*D*ear God, I long to change parts of my life that are no longer working, but don't know where to start. Help me break down these big, scary goals into small and achievable steps. Give me courage to put these plans into action and turn my life around!

*M*ake no little plans; they have no magic to stir men's blood.

—Daniel Burnham

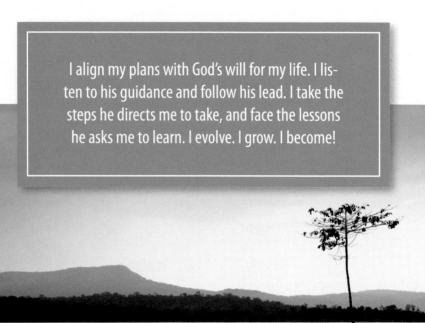

I align my plans with God's will for my life. I listen to his guidance and follow his lead. I take the steps he directs me to take, and face the lessons he asks me to learn. I evolve. I grow. I become!

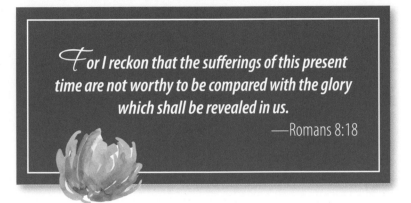

For I reckon that the sufferings of this present time are not worthy to be compared with the glory which shall be revealed in us.

—Romans 8:18

In the planning stages of a goal, it's hard to stay committed. There are so many distractions that steal our time and attention. But if we hold on for the long haul, our plans turn into achievements we can truly be proud of.

Whenever I make plans for anything in my life, I check with God in prayer first. If it rings true in my heart, which is where God speaks to me, I go for it. The ideas may be mine, but the inspiration and motivation to make them a reality come from God.

A man's heart deviseth his way: but the Lord directeth his steps.
—Proverbs 16:9

$\mathcal{F}$ather God, watch over me as I begin this new journey. I made my plans and created a blueprint for change. I now ask your help carrying it out in the world. Guide me along and help me adjust my path when my plans don't always pan out the way I hoped. Amen.

Dear God, today if I feel the urge to do something different, whether it's to explore a neighborhood park or museum, take a class, see a particular movie, or try a new kind of food, I will go for it. If it isn't a plausible idea for today, I will at least make plans to fit it in later this week or this month.

I know with God on my side, I cannot fail. The joyful plans I make for my goals and dreams are infused with his love and grace. All I do is listen for his voice within and I am on my way to a bold, new me!

*W*hat we desire must align with what God wants for us. Dreams fulfilled are dreams chosen by the one who knows us and loves us most. God always directs our plans to the outcome he knows is best.

*F*or I know the thoughts that I think toward you, saith the Lord, thoughts of peace, and not of evil, to give you an expected end.

—Jeremiah 29:11

*L*ast year, my friend Cynthia was involved in a freak accident that killed her mother Susan and later her husband Mike. The three were heading to a family wedding when a wheel assembly from a passing truck hit their car. Because of where she was sitting, Cynthia survived with minor injuries. Cynthia didn't know it at the time, but she was three weeks pregnant. She gave birth to a healthy baby boy and who is her pride and joy. "I don't think the accident was part of God's plan, but it helps to know that Mike lives on through my son and through the people who received Mike's organs," Cynthia says. God, when plans change in such life-altering ways, help us find silver linings.

My husband Ken and I recently bought our first house, a little brick bungalow with beautiful bay windows. We've lived in apartments up until now, and suddenly we are homeowners, with all that entails. It's been exciting to transform the little bungalow from a house into our home, and we've spent time and money in our efforts to do so. There are the practical purchases, like a small lawn mower, and then there are what Ken and I call "fun" purchases, like new curtains for the living room. There are many more things we'd like to do, but we work hard for our income, and know we need to pace ourselves financially. As Ken reminded me the other day, God instructs us to plan carefully down to the last detail, and calculate the costs of everything we do. Some things are going to have to wait, but in the meantime, we are wise to be happy with the fruits of our labors— the blessing of a new home.

*The fear of man bringeth a snare:
but whoso putteth his trust in the Lord
shall be safe.*

—Proverbs 29:25

When Ellie's son Jon was involved in an accident at age 8 that left him with the cognitive functioning of an infant, being his caretaker and tireless advocate became a major part of her life. She changed his diapers, administered liquid food and medicine through his feeding tube, lifted him in and out of his wheelchair, swam with him in a therapy pool, and brought him to church. When Jon died last year, nearly 15 years after his accident, it left a gaping hole in her life. If she was no longer Jon's caretaker, who was she? After her grief subsided, Ellie started making plans for this new chapter in her life. She still advocates for people with disabilities, counsels families in similar situations, volunteers with an organization working with children who have Down's syndrome, and talks about Jon often. "Talking about Jon ensures he won't be forgotten," Ellie says. Lord, when plans change, help us move forward with strength, always seeking out ways to make a difference in this world.

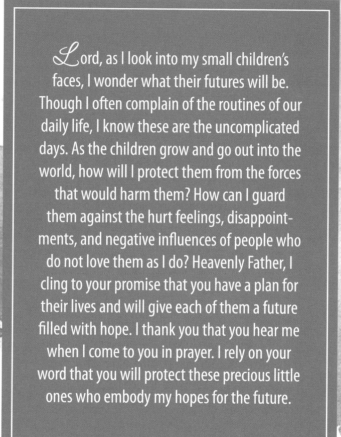

$\mathcal{L}$ord, as I look into my small children's faces, I wonder what their futures will be. Though I often complain of the routines of our daily life, I know these are the uncomplicated days. As the children grow and go out into the world, how will I protect them from the forces that would harm them? How can I guard them against the hurt feelings, disappointments, and negative influences of people who do not love them as I do? Heavenly Father, I cling to your promise that you have a plan for their lives and will give each of them a future filled with hope. I thank you that you hear me when I come to you in prayer. I rely on your word that you will protect these precious little ones who embody my hopes for the future.

*S*ometimes I am afraid. Sometimes the path before me seems almost impossible. Last year, I decided to return to school. The office where I work indicated that I would have a better chance of advancing if I pursued a graduate degree. But I was anxious. School has never come easily to me, and at this stage of my life, I have myriad responsibilities, including a house and two young children. But I prayed about it, and worked with my husband to figure out a humane course schedule that makes sense for our family. Though it will take a long time, I will eventually earn my degree. This first year I have been gratified to learn that I can keep up with my coursework and still make time for my job and family. It isn't always easy, though, and I pray for strength every day. I have learned that if I have faith, God will help me take on enormous challenges.

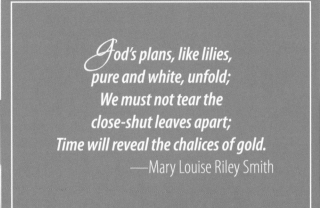

God's plans, like lilies,
pure and white, unfold;
We must not tear the
close-shut leaves apart;
Time will reveal the chalices of gold.

—Mary Louise Riley Smith

When you think of the term "success," what do you think of? Wealth? Fame? A Nobel Prize? Being realistic, only a small percentage of us will ever actually achieve this narrow definition of success. However, I sincerely believe each and every one of us can experience success in this life. It all depends on how you define it. And one of the surest paths to success is to figure out what your purpose is and go after it. Not as easy as it sounds, I know; but just acknowledging and beginning the process will make you feel more successful today than you were yesterday! Today, God, I will write down one thing I can realistically accomplish that will make me feel successful.

$\mathcal{A}$ few years ago I started a tradition for my birthday. Instead of hoping for gifts and attention, I took my birthday happiness in my own hands and spent the day giving others "gifts"—one for each year of my life. This year with my two daughters as my dates, we crisscrossed the city doing I-won't-tell-you-how-many random acts of kindness. They were just simple little things: mowing our elderly neighbor's lawn, adding coins to expired meters, picking up garbage at the park, delivering travel-size personal items to a homeless shelter, passing out a few movie gift cards at the mall, and handing out flowers to residents of a nursing home. As the day ended I was overflowing with happiness. It was the best birthday I have ever had. Lord, today I will plan a day where I will forget about whether it will make me happy or not and spend a day devoted to the happiness a loved one who has been having a rough time. I will put the day in my planner and hold myself accountable to deliver!

> $\mathcal{I}$ have learned...that if one advances confidently in the direction of his dreams, and endeavors to live the life which he has imagined, he will meet with a success unexpected in common hours.
>
> —Henry David Thoreau

*T*hroughout life, one of the hardest words to hear is WAIT. Sometimes we may anxiously wonder, "Where is God when I need him?" And yet we are reminded in Scripture, "Blessed are all they that wait for him" (Isaiah 30:18). Patience is developed through faithful waiting. God has a design in even the most difficult situations that will enable our character to become stronger. As we learn patience, we also learn to trust that God has our best interests in mind. He cannot abandon us, and he will always rescue us at just the right time.

*A*nd therefore will the Lord wait, that he may be gracious unto you, and therefore will he be exalted, that he may have mercy upon you: for the Lord is a God of judgment: blessed are all they that wait for him.

—Isaiah 30:18

MY AIM IS...
to please him through communing in prayer
to show his love and for others care
to read his Word as my guide for life
to cease my grumbling that causes strife
to be open to God's leading and his will
to take time to meditate, be quiet, and still
to continually grow in my Christlike walk
to be more like Jesus in my life and my talk.

Heavenly Father, I ask for your bright presence. Protect me from the worldly hurts and evils that sometimes cloud life. Help me forget the past, look to the future, and be eager for new starts. Replace darkness and doubt with the light of your love. Forgive me, so I might forgive others. Amen.

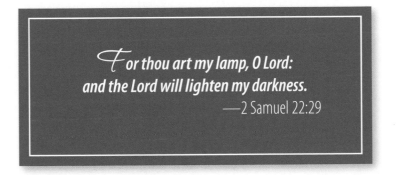

For thou art my lamp, O Lord:
and the Lord will lighten my darkness.
—2 Samuel 22:29

For God so loved the world, that he gave his only begotten Son, that whosoever believeth in him should not perish, but have everlasting life.

—John 3:16

For all the things we have to be grateful for in this life, one of the most encouraging for us as children of God is that the best is yet to come. Our time here is just a warm-up for what lies ahead. Everything on the earth that is marked by decay, decline, disease, and death will no longer exist in heaven. God will bring Christ's victory to fullness when he does away with the old and ushers us into the new. Give thanks with all your heart today, for no matter what your pain, loss, failure, or fear might be, in Christ you have victory over it and a glorious future beyond it! Dear Lord, grant that I may keep an eternal perspective from which I can thank you for the best that is yet to come.

Chapter 10

STAND UP

✦

We will know when it's time to make our stand. God will speak to us a little louder, a little stronger. The whisper within will become a mighty roar, as we are encouraged to step out in faith and be who God meant us to be.

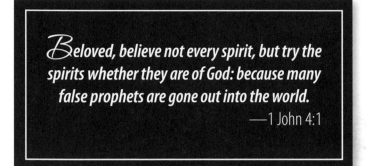

Beloved, believe not every spirit, but try the spirits whether they are of God: because many false prophets are gone out into the world.

—1 John 4:1

God, give me the insight to discern your will for me. Help me to ignore those who may not have my best interests at heart.
Give me strength to stay on my own path until I achieve my goals.

A s soon as I stand up in God's light, I am given the power I need to move mountains. As soon as I move forward in faith, the challenges and obstacles in my way disappear. I can overcome anything with God as my ally.

*T*hen ye shall rise up from the ambush, and seize upon the city: for the Lord your God will deliver it into your hand.

—Joshua 8:7

And I will raise me up a faithful priest, that shall do according to that which is in mine heart and in my mind: and I will build him a sure house.

—1 Samuel 2:35

Dear God, I rise each day in the power of your love, knowing I can accomplish anything. I rise each day in joy feeling your will move through me, knowing I can achieve all things.

*G*od helps those who help themselves. We are trained to believe we don't deserve to help ourselves, and that others always come first. But God demands we take care of our own needs, and make ourselves strong, happy, and hopeful first, so we can then help others do the same.

When I feel weak, tired, and alone, give me strength, God, to stand up and face the challenges before me with hope, grace, and the power that comes from your presence.

Help me, God, to find the courageous lion within.

The first step is always the hardest. Starting some-thing new requires we find the courage to overcome fear and doubt, and get out of our comfort zones. God is there for us, ready to take our hands and pull us up from where are to where we want to be.

If I remain small, whom do I serve? Certainly not God, who created me to be big and bold and authentic. Certainly not the world, which needs my creative fire and loving spirit. Certainly not myself, with so much to live for and offer.
Let me be big, bold, and authentic!

Though you may be afraid, you've got the power of God on your side. So stand up and be the fullest and deepest expression of yourself you can possibly be. Let God do his will in your life and light up the world with your brilliance, your talents, and the gifts only you can give.

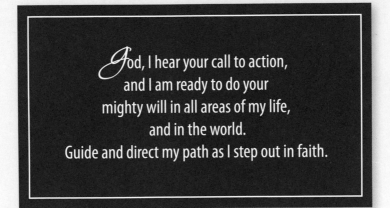

God, I hear your call to action,
and I am ready to do your
mighty will in all areas of my life,
and in the world.
Guide and direct my path as I step out in faith.

*F*ather, it's easy to say, "Let me know if there's anything I can do." But how much better to peer closer, assess the situation to find what needs doing—then simply do it. Help me look into a friend's needs instead of waiting to be asked. Help me replace the words I utter so glibly with actions that might matter even more. Amen.

*T*hen the disciples, every man according to his ability, determined to send relief unto the brethren which dwelt in Judaea.

—Acts 11:29

When the despair that comes with the pain of a loss immobilizes us and makes us feel powerless, God gives us the inner fortitude and grace we need to stand up, get over the suffering, and get on with our lives.

One test of people's character is what they do in hard times—what they do under pressure. Do they compromise their integrity using excuses for their wrong choices? Or do they have the courage to stand up and do the right thing no matter what they come up against?

*D*ear God, the news of my illness terrified me, and I am feeling lost and afraid. I come to you asking for your healing and comfort as I go forward in dealing with my diagnosis. Without your support and love, God, I am sure I won't be able to withstand the treatments and anxiety and fear, not just for myself, but for my family. In your arms I seek caring and mercy and the strength I need to return to good health. In your presence I know I will find my way, and move towards a renewal of body, mind, and spirit. Help me, oh God, to stand against this challenge, and win. Amen.

*H*eal me, O Lord, and I shall be healed; save me, and I shall be saved: for thou art my praise.
—Jeremiah 17:14

By doing good, and doing it with love, we can overcome anything. It is such a simple way to live, but it works when we stay the course and let God do his will through us and for us. We can choose to be a part of the problem, or a part of the solution, and that choice might mean looking beyond the difficulties of life and showing gratitude for the sheer fact we are alive. Changing perspective and putting our lives back into the hands of a loving God can make all the difference. God, I ask that my will become yours and that I do all things through the same love you've unceasingly shown me. Let me be an example of how choosing love is choosing right.

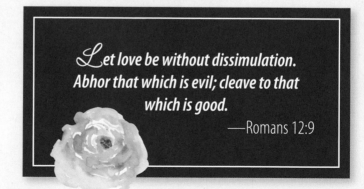

Let love be without dissimulation. Abhor that which is evil; cleave to that which is good.

—Romans 12:9

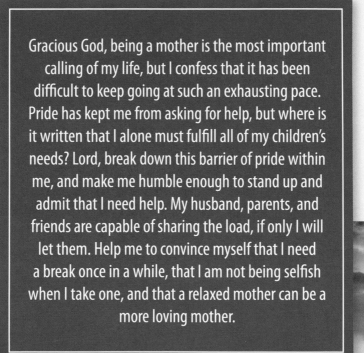

Gracious God, being a mother is the most important calling of my life, but I confess that it has been difficult to keep going at such an exhausting pace. Pride has kept me from asking for help, but where is it written that I alone must fulfill all of my children's needs? Lord, break down this barrier of pride within me, and make me humble enough to stand up and admit that I need help. My husband, parents, and friends are capable of sharing the load, if only I will let them. Help me to convince myself that I need a break once in a while, that I am not being selfish when I take one, and that a relaxed mother can be a more loving mother.

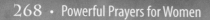

*S*he is like the merchants' ships;
she bringeth her food from afar.
—Proverbs 31:14

The recession hit our family hard, but I'm proud of the way my husband and I stepped up and managed what could have been a scary situation. I've worked outside the home since our children were small, but after the market collapse, my husband was laid off and we both took on a series of extra jobs to make ends meet. It wasn't always easy, but together, we have stayed on top of the bills and kept things stable for the kids. I see the same grit in my sister, who is a young widow with a son of her own. "Women are strong," I tell her, and I mean it.

**Dear Lord, thank you for this strength.
Women are providers!**

Feel the fear and do it anyway, for you will find you have more inner strength than you ever imagined. Call upon God to be there, should you fall, and go ahead and try. You may find out that you had the ability to do it alone all along, but isn't it good to know that when you can't, God is there to back you up?

Like a toddler who falls more than he stands, I'm pulling myself upright in the aftermath of death. I know you as a companion, God of mending hearts, and feel you steadying me. Thank you for the gift of resilience. Lead me to others who have hurt and gone on; I need to see how it's done.

*W*hen you examine your daily life, what evidence of the past do you see? Many of the great inventors, writers, teachers, builders, and artists who passed away long ago made contributions that have survived long after their deaths. Perhaps future generations will not remember us specifically by name, but we can at least each contribute to something that will live on, whether by volunteering for a venerable organization or being the best parent or teacher we can be so our children or pupils change the world for the better. Focus on beautiful, lasting details rather than passing trends that change every other week. God, remind me to spend time doing something that will outlast me. Perhaps I will plant a tree or get more involved in local recycling efforts.

*N*othing pulls on the heartstrings more than the sight of a child who is hungry or hurting. Children are our future, and each one has such potential. When any of them suffer, our hopes for the future dim a little. Lord, today I will reach out to help a child in need by volunteering at my local children's hospital or at a homeless shelter that serves families with children.

If any of you lack wisdom, let him ask of God, that giveth to all men liberally, and upbraideth not; and it shall be given him.

—James 1:5

I recently took on a new position at work. It's a stretch for me, and while I welcome the change (my previous duties no longer challenged me), I am also fearful of failure. My new position will require a steep learning curve, and demands that I oversee a number of employees. What if I can't master the material? What if I don't have what it takes to manage others wisely? But I must remember that God is always there to help me. He can increase wisdom—not just spiritually, but in all ways. Dear Lord, please be with me as I challenge myself to develop intellectually and master new skills. Please help me to stay sharp, and to grow as a person, with energy and grace.

Trust in the Lord, and do good; so shalt thou dwell in the land, and verily thou shalt be fed.

—Psalm 37:3

*F*aith is a commodity that cannot be purchased, traded, or sold. It is a treasure that cannot be claimed and put on display in a museum. It is a richness no amount of money can compare to. When you have faith, you have a power that can change night into day, move mountains, calm stormy seas. When you have faith, you can fall over and over again, only to stand up each time more determined than ever to succeed, and you will succeed. For faith is God in action, and faith is available to anyone—rich, poor, young, or old—as long as you believe.

𝓛ord, I wish to live a long life, but I fear growing old. I want to accomplish great things, but I fear risking what I already have. I desire to love with all my heart, but the prospect of self-revelation makes me shrink back. Perhaps for just this day, you would help me reach out? Let me bypass these dreads and see your hand reaching back to mine—right now—just as it always has.

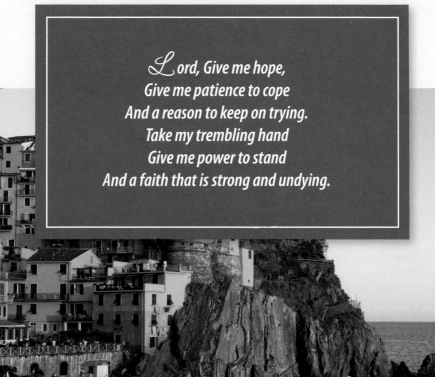

𝓛ord, Give me hope,
Give me patience to cope
And a reason to keep on trying.
Take my trembling hand
Give me power to stand
And a faith that is strong and undying.

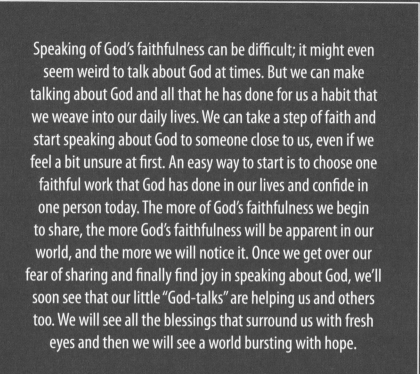

Speaking of God's faithfulness can be difficult; it might even seem weird to talk about God at times. But we can make talking about God and all that he has done for us a habit that we weave into our daily lives. We can take a step of faith and start speaking about God to someone close to us, even if we feel a bit unsure at first. An easy way to start is to choose one faithful work that God has done in our lives and confide in one person today. The more of God's faithfulness we begin to share, the more God's faithfulness will be apparent in our world, and the more we will notice it. Once we get over our fear of sharing and finally find joy in speaking about God, we'll soon see that our little "God-talks" are helping us and others too. We will see all the blessings that surround us with fresh eyes and then we will see a world bursting with hope.

*D*ear Lord, my role as a parent puts me in a commanding position. Children have little power, and it is up to me, as my child's guardian, to be a helpmeet and advocate in a world that is not always just. My son, who is nine, has been dealing with a bully at school. I've had to go in to meet with the principal and the other boy's parents several times, and the parents have on more than one occasion grown belligerent. It's an uncomfortable situation, but I know I must remain strong and level headed in order to support my child. God, please grant me the strength to always do what is right for my child, even at risk of personal discomfort, as the parents of Moses did.

> *B*y faith Moses, when he was born, was hid three months of his parents, because they saw he was a proper child; and they were not afraid of the king's commandment.
>
> —Hebrews 11:23

> *Let your light so shine before men, that they may see your good works, and glorify your Father which is in heaven.*
> —Matthew 5:16

I am by nature a quiet and reserved person; like my parents before me, I've always believed actions speak louder than words. When our pastor recently gave a sermon challenging the congregation to go out and share with others the way God has helped us grow, I initially felt resistant. "Not my style!" was my knee-jerk reaction. And yet talking with the pastor after the service, I realized that showing reverence to God could take different forms. I don't have to go out and preach about how God has helped me improve myself. I can simply demonstrate growth through my actions, whether I'm quitting smoking or getting better at managing my temper. If people ask, as someone recently did, "How did you quit smoking?" I can always give a simple answer: "Prayer." Lord, I can demonstrate my beliefs and inspire others by always striving to better myself. Please help me stand up to honor you in this way.

*C*ivilization means different things to different people. To me, it means maintaining a certain order and level of decency. Though the civilization we live in is far from achieving equal respect for all people, we can make progress every day, and I can certainly encourage progress in my own community. Today I will encourage equal respect for all people in my community. If I notice a wrong, heavenly Father, I will work to make it right. If I encounter a homeless person I will buy him a meal or I will donate my time or money to a cause that helps people who are less fortunate than I am.

Most of us are expert procrastinators; I know I am. If you are anything like me, you can think of numerous things to do to get you out of the matter in front of you. We worry for days (or weeks, or longer!) about something that, in the end, takes only a few hours to finish. Maybe if we can focus on the satisfaction and relief of finally getting a procrastinated task done, we will be quicker to jump in and do it the next time. Today, Lord, I will pick one thing I have been putting off, and I will get started on it.

Chapter 11

PUSH THROUGH

✴

God, let me thank you for all of the times you've pushed me forward when I wanted to stop. For the days when I thought I could not continue, thank you for giving me the shove I needed to break on through. With you, I can go on and fight the good fight!

If you find stumbling blocks in your path, use them as stepping-stones to move closer to the good in life.

I will not turn back. I will not give up. I will never surrender. With God at my side, I will simply step over obstacles, go around challenges, and break through blocks put in my path. With God, I am unstoppable!

When everyone seems against us, we must remember God is for us! Victory in life comes to those who know that, no matter how many times our enemies attack, we will win with God as our ally.

My times are in thy hand: deliver me from the hand of mine enemies, and from them that persecute me.

—Psalm 31:15

*S*ometimes our children, spouses, family, and friends take a toll on our energy. We feel we have given all we have to give. This is the time to step away, get quiet with God, and recharge the batteries so we can push on through another day.

For whatsoever is born of God overcometh the world: and this is the victory that overcometh the world, even our faith.

—1 John 5:4

When I operate from my own will, I grow tired and weary. When I accept God's will, I feel as though the floodgates have opened and I am floating downstream, relaxed and in the flow of blessings.

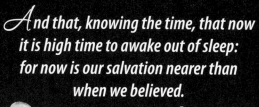

And that, knowing the time, that now it is high time to awake out of sleep: for now is our salvation nearer than when we believed.

—Romans 13:11

*W*omen work hard, and often we want to do nothing but sleep for days. But God asks that we be awake and ready to lead, for we are the nurturing force in a world so desperately in need of compassion and love.

A happy attitude is food for the spirit. Staying in God's grace makes the challenges of life a little easier. Lessons are learned with less effort. Mercy is given more freely. Joy returns!

The best way to deal with the pressures of everyday life is to patiently rely on God.

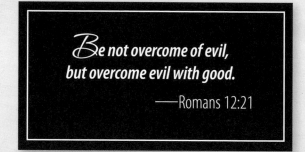

Be not overcome of evil,
but overcome evil with good.

—Romans 12:21

*G*od, teach me to have the courage to act in the
world as you wish me to. Help me find a way to
push through the challenges that arise in my path,
and show me how to overcome evil with love and
compassion. Help me to stand tall against fear and
stay in the light. Amen.

*F*ather God, in you I find comfort and peace after a day of working hard and pushing forward to reach my goals. In you I find strength when I've done all I can do on my own. In you I find my spirit renewed. Amen.

*L*ife goes back and forth between push and pull, force and acceptance, fight and surrender. It's exhausting! But staying in God's will makes the doors of life open easier and more frequently than when we rely only on ourselves.

*I*f you are faced with a roadblock in your life, how do you react? Are you immediately deflated, or does it spark your mind to come up with a solution to the problem at hand? Feeling deflated is the easy response, but we owe it to ourselves to summon our confidence and push through. No matter who we are, at some point in our lives we have tasted success at something, whether we are a whiz with numbers or excel at athletics or have the compassion it takes to go into the social work or medical fields. While we are not all as smart or talented as Albert Einstein or Michael Jordan, we all have talents and gifts we can strengthen and hone. Lord, help me push through any difficult circumstance by putting my unique gifts and talents to use.

My husband and I have encountered a rough patch in our marriage. Our youngest child recently began college, and transitioning to an "empty nest" home has been harder on us both than we anticipated. My husband, who misses our sons, has started a new job. He's not home as much just as I've begun contemplating taking retirement. So many days we seem to be at cross-purposes—we seem to want different things! But this morning when we sat down together over coffee, my husband reminded me that over the years, we have weathered many storms in our marriage—job loss, the deaths of our parents, our middle son's struggles with schoolwork and drugs. Each time we have prevailed together. It was a good conversation, and I think we felt closer to one another than we have in months. Dear Lord, you have joined my husband and me. You have blessed our partnership. To succeed, we must push through the present rough patch and take the long view!

What therefore God hath joined together, let not man put asunder.

—Mark 10:9

*T*he Spirit of God will guide us. All the stress goes out of navigating unknown territory when you have a guide. The guide knows all the best places to go, the shortcuts, the scenic routes, and the places to avoid. For our guide in life, God has given us his Spirit. The unknown future lies before us at every moment, but it is not unknown to God. His Spirit will lead us if we'll accept his guidance. "If we live in the Spirit," Paul said, "let us also walk in the Spirit" (Galatians 5:25).

Follow God's Spirit, and you can't go wrong.

*D*ear God, I seek a little extra strength to get me through these tough days. Things are not going well, but I know that with your assistance, I can get through to the other side and thrive. Power me up to power me through, God! Amen.

We often need to patiently endure time and experience in order to be fully prepared for whatever God has planned for our lives.

God, I know that you close some doors in my life in order to open new ones. I know that things change and come to an end in order to leave room for new beginnings. Help me have the boldness and enthusiasm to let go of the old and accept the new. Amen.

I remember someone saying that what doesn't make us bitter will make us better. Lord, I've never seen the good in becoming bitter about life. Your grace is always big enough for each of us, whether our trials are few or many. I want to become better, though, when I come through a painful struggle, a difficulty, or a loss. Help me remember that the work of making me better is your work. My work is to remain faithful to you—trusting in you. From within that place of trust, you will fashion a better kind of faith, hope, and love within me.

*M*oney is a big issue for most people, and I am no exception. Either we don't have enough, or we worry about losing what we have. We are afraid of being left homeless and destitute. But God promises he will comfort and nourish us, with material things and things no amount of money can buy. God tells us not to be afraid. Dear God, I pray to worry less, and have more faith in your promise of prosperity. Even when my wallet looks empty, I know that blessings are happening in the unseen and will soon be made manifest. You never fail to sustain and support me, God. I pray for your care and comfort in good financial times and in bad.

> *N*ow therefore fear ye not: I will nourish you, and your little ones. And he comforted them, and spake kindly unto them.
> —Genesis 50:21

$\mathscr{L}$ord, we understand that there are and will be problems in our lives, but please remind us of your presence when the problems seem insurmountable. We want to believe that you know best. We hope to remain patient as we search for purpose. Amen.

Life is scary, if we really think about it (or perhaps overthink about it!). Even the "good" days hold moments of worry or uncertainty. But the uncertainty is what keeps each day new and exciting. If we let fear hold us back, we will miss out on so many wonderful experiences. Sure, we may lose or end up hurt, but we also may win or be blessed with utter joy. So much of life is about just moving forward. If you let fear hold you back, you will never know how good things could have been or what dreams you could have achieved. If I find myself feeling afraid today, God, help me stand firm and push through the fear. I can push through anything when I have you by my side.

*J*ust when all seems hopeless, prayer lifts us like a wave on the ocean. A sturdy craft, prayer doesn't hide from pain, but uses it like the force of the sea to move us to a new place of insight, patience, courage, and sympathy. Always, it is God's hand beneath the surface holding us up.

*L*ord, today I pray for all those who are suffering from any sort of addiction. Whether it's drugs, gambling, overeating, or compulsive exercising, Lord, addiction keeps them from being the people you designed them to be. Their obsession separates them from you and walls them off from their loved ones as well. Break through and release them from their chains, Lord. Give them the strength to put their troubles behind them and find new life in you.

Some years ago, I moved from a big city that offered public transportation out to the suburbs, where I needed to drive a car to get around. It wasn't long before I discovered I had a temper quick to respond to being cut off, or tailgated, or any other of a number of driving irritations. Hello, road rage. Eventually my friends and family noticed my bad mood after every commute, and I realized that I was creating my own unhappiness. Then one day I was driving home from the pet store with a new guppy bound for my fish tank, taking it slowly, driving gingerly over the railroad tracks. When other drivers responded with irritation and honking, I realized that no one really knows what another person is experiencing, and instead of anger, it would be wiser to reserve judgment and respond with compassion, patience, and calm. Good-bye, road rage! Whether driving, negotiating a crowded store, or dealing with a business phone call, it's good to assume the best intentions and respect others' feelings and experiences. God, when faced with a frustrating situation, remind me to take a deep breath, assume the best in others, and let go of anger.

God, grant me the courage to let go of shame, guilt, and anger. Free me of all negative energies, for only then will I become a conduit for joy and a channel for goodness. Amen.

It is not always easy to understand others; it is not always easy to understand oneself! This came home to me last week, when I "woke up on the wrong side of the bed." From the moment I got up to make coffee, I was filled with a pervasive sense of anxiety. I tried to take care, giving myself extra time for my commute to work, and organizing my day to minimize stress. And yet nothing seemed to help until I had the sense to close my office door, put my phone aside, and say the quiet, simple prayer, "Help." I won't tell you that my anxiety magically went away; it didn't. But I had a moment to collect myself, to register some of the things that had piled up throughout the week—a bad grade my son earned in math, the leaky faucet, the fact that I haven't been sleeping as well—and the understanding gave me some context, and consequently some relief. Understanding our own concerns is a part of our ongoing education as to who we are as people. God, you have the power to look into my mind and soul to know what causes my anxiety. Thank you for helping me to remember that. Thank you for being there to guide me.

$\mathcal{I}$ am an emergency room nurse and love my job, which can be by turns intense, interesting, and challenging. No two days are alike, though much of the time I am invited to think on my feet. I do like that aspect of the job. But lately, the ER has been so busy that by shift's end I find myself exhausted, both mentally and physically. I must remember that what I do has value, and these things run in cycles. I've worked long enough to understand that the pace will eventually settle, at least temporarily, and that I mustn't let a hard day of work get me down. Dear God, help me to take the long view. Remind me on the days when my spirits and energy are low, that ultimately things always get better.

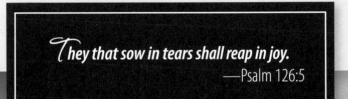

They that sow in tears shall reap in joy.
—Psalm 126:5

*M*isfortune is no respecter of persons. Trouble and hardship do not discriminate. Face it—misfortune is bound to happen to each of us. If we accept that adversity will happen, we can decide, here and now, to face it with as much courage and optimism as we can muster. Often we don't think much about how we will handle adversity until it is upon us. But much like a muscle that strengthens with use, we can "bulk up" our optimism and our courage to prepare in advance for how we will face—and conquer—the challenges that lie ahead. Today, God, I will spend time exercising my optimism muscle! I will give every challenge my best effort.

My grandfather always used to say, "We have to play the hand we were dealt." It took me a long time to understand that this saying simply meant that our job is to take what life gave us and do the best we can with it. We don't choose our family, our nationality, or even our gender, but we can use our unique set of circumstances as a jumping-off point for an amazing life story! Lord, I promise to make good choices and make the most of my circumstances, talents, and opportunities.

Our real blessings often appear to us in the shape of pains, losses and disappointments; but let us have patience, and we soon shall see them in their proper figures.

——Joseph Addison

Change is never easy, but the blessings it bestows upon us are magnificent. Just ask the caterpillar struggling within the tight confines of a cocoon. Even as it struggles, it is becoming something glorious, something beautiful, soon to emerge as a winged butterfly. Change may bring temporary pain and discomfort, but it also brings the promise of a new life filled with joy and freedom and the ability to soar even higher than we ever did before.

Gracious God, I turn to you when I am feeling lost and alone.
You restore me with strength and hope and the courage to face
a new day. You bless me with joy and comfort me through trials
and tribulations. You direct my thoughts, guide my actions, and
temper my words. You give me the patience and kindness I need
to be good. Gracious God, I turn to you. Amen.

*L*ord, our situations and circumstances may look
pretty bleak, but when we take time to look at the
accomplishments of others who have persevered,
we can take heart and have courage.

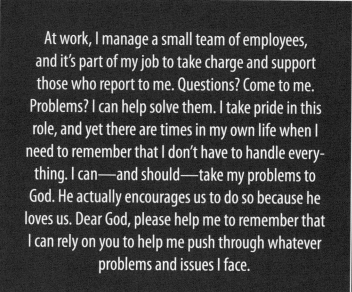

At work, I manage a small team of employees, and it's part of my job to take charge and support those who report to me. Questions? Come to me. Problems? I can help solve them. I take pride in this role, and yet there are times in my own life when I need to remember that I don't have to handle everything. I can—and should—take my problems to God. He actually encourages us to do so because he loves us. Dear God, please help me to remember that I can rely on you to help me push through whatever problems and issues I face.

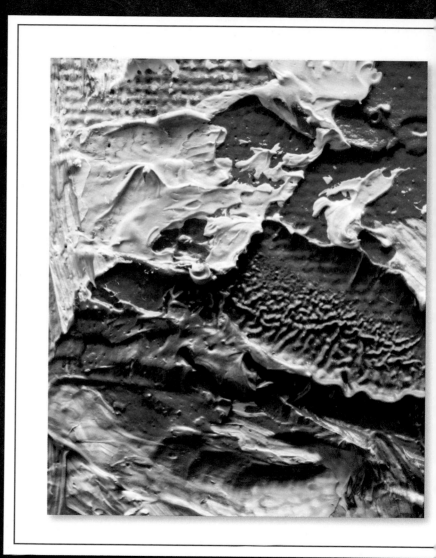

Chapter 12

BE YOURSELF

God, you have called each of us to special tasks, purposes, and vocations, equipping us with the skills and energy to perform them. For some, our vocations send us into the labor force; for some, it is soon bringing retirement. For some, it is in full-time homemaking. For some, our vocations are in artistic skills; for some, in volunteering, helping, neighboring. Always, there is that first call from you, God of vision, working through us to help, heal, change a needful world.

*S*o God created man in his own image,
in the image of God created he him;
male and female created he them.
—Genesis 1:27

"I'm fat," Lauren's 13-year-old daughter Gwen announced unhappily at breakfast one morning. "Trish at school said so." Lauren finished preparing their eggs, then sat down with her daughter. "You are not fat," she said. "And Trish sounds like an unhappy person." As Gwen finished her breakfast and started to gather her school things, Lauren gave her a hug. "God created you in his image, which is a pretty amazing thing," she said. "Don't ever forget you are *beautiful*." Dear God, on days when I am low, help me to accept myself. May I always remember that you made me in your own image!

*W*hen Angela's son Kevin left for college, Angela was surprised to discover the extent to which she felt at loose ends. "I was still working as a nurse then," she remembers, "but with Kevin successfully out in the world, I felt a lack of motivation." Reexamining her faith helped. "I began by thanking God for Kevin's happiness—the way he was spreading his wings," she says now. "Glorifying God in this way restored to me a feeling of purpose." God, when I'm feeling down about myself and my purpose in life, may I remember to glorify you—*that* is my purpose!

*E*ven every one that is called by my name: for I have created him for my glory, I have formed him; yea, I have made him.

—Isaiah 43:7

For who maketh thee to differ from another? and what hast thou that thou didst not receive? now if thou didst receive it, why dost thou glory, as if thou hadst not received it?

—1 Corinthians 4:7

Stephanie's two sons are as different as night and day. Jon is quiet, thoughtful, and a quick study in math. His younger brother Mark is an ebullient artist. Stephanie, who tries to make sure that each boy is recognized within the family, also encourages them to appreciate what their sibling brings to the table. "I try to instill in them a feeling of confidence in their particular gifts," Stephanie says, "even as they recognize and celebrate another's talents." Dear God, you grant us unique gifts that make us different. May we glorify and celebrate those differences in one another!

*M*indy was horrified when her daughter Natalie and a friend made fun of a man standing farther down the subway platform. "The girls were snickering about his shoes, which were held together with tape," Mindy says. "I told them it is never okay to judge those who lack." Years later, Natalie also remembers the incident. "Mom was gentle but firm: she let me know in no uncertain terms that my behavior was unacceptable. I learned something that day!"

Dear Lord, may I live in a way that respects others. May I show by my actions that each person has value.

*W*hoso mocketh the poor reproacheth his Maker: and he that is glad at calamities shall not be unpunished.

—Proverbs 17:5

*T*abitha's sister Ellen struggles with debilitating shyness. "I try to remember to compliment Ellen sincerely," Tabitha says. "It's very hard for her to socialize with people she doesn't know, and then she gets down on herself. But I tell her, 'You have a tremendous sense of personal style. You are the most interesting-looking person in the room!' I figure, why not remind her of how cool she is? It's true!" Lord, I can help others through praise. May I encourage self-acceptance by building someone else up today.

> *I* will praise thee; for I am fearfully and wonderfully made: marvellous are thy works; and that my soul knoweth right well.
> —Psalm 139:14

Fear ye not therefore, ye are of more value than many sparrows.

—Matthew 10:31

Helen, a 70-year-old widow, stays active and enjoys a wide circle of friends, her two sons, and her grandkids. But sometimes, her body reminds her of the passage of time. "I have a little arthritis," she admits. "Some days it slows me down; it bothers me when I have to ask my kids for help. But then I remember: I'm still me, even with arthritis. My kids love me. And so does God!" Dear God, I am growing older. My body is not as strong as it used to be; sometimes I feel like a burden. But you tell us we are valued, always—please help me to remember this!

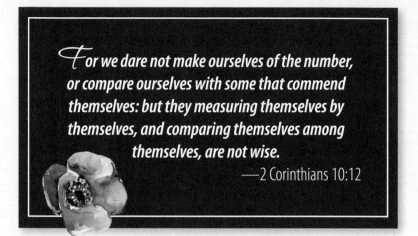

For we dare not make ourselves of the number, or compare ourselves with some that commend themselves: but they measuring themselves by themselves, and comparing themselves among themselves, are not wise.

—2 Corinthians 10:12

When Miranda first tried yoga, her classmates, some of whom had been practicing for years, intimidated her. But her instructor, Jane, helped put things in perspective. "Jane reminded me that yoga isn't about comparing oneself to others," Miranda says. "It's about my own progress. I may never be as flexible as some of my classmates, but I'm proud of the improvements I've seen in my own abilities." Dear Lord, sometimes I fall into the trap of comparing myself to others, and that's a slippery slope. Help me to focus on my own progress, my own heart—not someone else's.

"I have a temper," Therese admits; her short fuse is something she has worked on for much of her life. "I'd been making progress, but then my son Gary turned 15 and we started butting heads *all the time!*" she shares. "I was discouraged by the setback, but I'm trying hard to respond to Gary in a different, more positive way. With God's help, I know I can continue to grow: as a parent, and as a person." God, I am a work in progress, and with your help I will continue to grow. Help me to face setbacks in my personal evolution with courage and good humor.

"Two steps forward, one step back. Sometimes I get discouraged!" Ava says with a laugh. She's talking about her efforts to be more organized at work. "My desk still gets really messy sometimes—I'm terrible about filing things away and I get these piles of paper everywhere—but I remind myself that I'm on the right path. My performance at work has improved overall." She smiles wryly. "There is hope!"

Dear Lord, help me to have confidence that I am on the right path as I strive to grow as a person.

And we know that all things work together for good to them that love God, to them who are the called according to his purpose.
—Romans 8:28

*A*s the mother of a young child, I naturally cross paths with other moms—some work outside the home, and some are stay-at-home moms, like me. At this time of my life, staying home with my baby is the right choice for our family, but I respect those who make a different choice. I have been surprised and disappointed at how vehemently mothers on both sides of the home-or-work question have criticized what they see as the "incorrect" path. My best girlfriend, a mom of two, works full-time, and both of us have encountered criticisms from those who make claims about who we are as people based on our choice in this matter. It can be hard not to become defensive, and my friend feels the same. Lord, help us to be unconcerned when the world tries to define us. Help us to access strength and our best selves through spirituality.

When Donna counseled her 15-year-old daughter, Bette, to reach out in kindness to others, she was thinking of the good Bette might do—and also the way her daughter would benefit. "She's a good kid, but self-absorbed right now," Donna says. "I want Bette to look beyond herself. She's been feeling bad about herself, and I know from my own experience that by uplifting others, Bette will also feel better in her own heart. I want that for her." Dear God, I honor you when I celebrate and uplift others. I also honor myself. By loving, I become more beautiful and whole.

He that hath my commandments, and keepeth them, he it is that loveth me: and he that loveth me shall be loved of my Father, and I will love him, and will manifest myself to him.

—John 14:21

Teaching us that, denying ungodliness and worldly lusts, we should live soberly, righteously, and godly, in this present world.
—Titus 2:12

*H*ave you ever met someone who solely defines themselves by their possessions? Though society may seem to reward those who achieve their self-worth from having the "right" car, or the biggest house, these individuals are, at the root of it, unhappy people. Material gain in and of itself is, ultimately, an empty victory. Don't be that person. Don't let your worldly interests cloud your true sense of self.

Dear God, may what *really* matters define who I am as a person!

*Then said Jesus unto his disciples,
If any man will come after me,
let him deny himself, and take up his cross,
and follow me. For whosoever will save his
life shall lose it: and whosoever will lose his
life for my sake shall find it.*

—Matthew 16:24–25

$\mathcal{A}$ few days after retiring, Violet visited the local hospital and asked how she could be of service. Her kids were grown, and she and her husband had divorced a decade ago. She wanted to define a new way to make a difference. "My volunteer work fulfills me," she says now. "I feel I am manifesting Christ's teachings when I help others; serving God in this way helps me realize my best self." Dear Lord, may I always remember that self-realization is achieved through my service to you.

> *But the fruit of the Spirit is love, joy, peace, longsuffering, gentleness, goodness, faith.*
> —Galatians 5:22

As an adult with many demands on my time and energy, I am always interested in how to consistently achieve my potential and be my best self. For many years, I've enjoyed swimming as a way to stay healthy, both physically and emotionally. After a long day, a good swim clears my head, tones my muscles, and keeps me sharp and upbeat. Similarly, I've found that staying spiritually active has a positive affect on my outlook. Like exercise, staying spiritually engaged takes discipline—and sometimes I would rather just sit on the couch and eat chips! But when I make the effort, physical and spiritual exercise helps me to realize joy. Lord, please may I always remember that happiness can be part of the package when I develop my spiritual muscle. I can "work at" making joy a constant in my life.

$\mathcal{A}$s a college student living in the United States, I have many advantages, and it's easy to fall into the trap of feeling that, given all I have going for me, I should "be the best at everything." I am hard on myself when I don't get the best grade, for example, or when I perceive that I'm not as physically attractive as some of the girls in the dorm. God, help me to remember that there is always room for improvement, a condition I share with everyone else on Earth, and that your Word can comfort me, guide me, and serve as the ultimate "self-improvement manual."

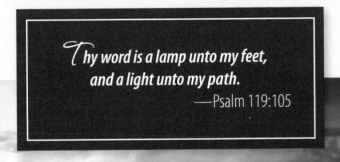

$\mathcal{T}$hy word is a lamp unto my feet,
and a light unto my path.
—Psalm 119:105

God of the strong and the weak, the brave and the fearful, I come before you to place myself in your loving hands. Take my broken places and make them whole. Heal my wounds that I might be strong for you. Give me patience to accept your timing, and help me to trust in your goodness. In your gracious name, I pray. Amen.

*M*arriage does not ask that you completely lose yourself in the other person. Remember, happy individuals make happy couples. Marriage does not demand that you think and act just like one another. Remember, it was your unique qualities that attracted you to each other in the first place. Marriage only requires that each of you becomes not someone else, but more of who you are already, only now you will become who you are together.

*B*ear ye one another's burdens,
and so fulfil the law of Christ.
—Galatians 6:2

Lord, I come to you boldly and gladly. Accept me as your child, and meet my needs. Amen.

*F*ather, you have enriched my life with many identities—daughter, friend, wife, and mother. Richness and joy have followed me through each phase of my life, and I have wholeheartedly accepted and enjoyed each role. But you knew, didn't you, Lord, that the title of mother would make such a strong claim on my heart? How I praise you for the greatest of your gifts, my children, and for the fulfillment they have brought. I need no other affirmation than to be called mother. My children have taught me to forget myself, and through them, I have learned what it means to be your child.

> *L*o, children are an heritage of the Lord: and the fruit of the womb is his reward.
>
> —Psalm 127:3

*D*ear Lord, teach my children to follow my lead in actions and deeds and to model my behavior more so than my words. Often I speak in frustration, but I always act in patience, kindness, and love. I want the same for my children. Help them do as I do, not as I say. Help my husband see beyond my occasional sharp or impatient words, my words of confusion, fear, and annoyance when things aren't going the way I would like. Help him to see the love I give, the work I do, the way I live and move and have my being. Amen.

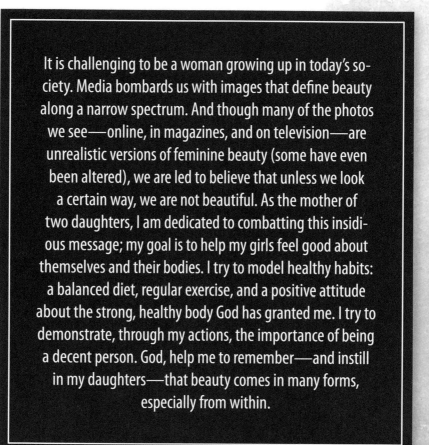

It is challenging to be a woman growing up in today's society. Media bombards us with images that define beauty along a narrow spectrum. And though many of the photos we see—online, in magazines, and on television—are unrealistic versions of feminine beauty (some have even been altered), we are led to believe that unless we look a certain way, we are not beautiful. As the mother of two daughters, I am dedicated to combatting this insidious message; my goal is to help my girls feel good about themselves and their bodies. I try to model healthy habits: a balanced diet, regular exercise, and a positive attitude about the strong, healthy body God has granted me. I try to demonstrate, through my actions, the importance of being a decent person. God, help me to remember—and instill in my daughters—that beauty comes in many forms, especially from within.

Creator God, I've been so busy being a mother, I've neglected my own creativity. I thought it was the right thing to do, but lately I've felt the urge to stretch my talents. Lord, please guide me. I feel guilty about wanting to do something for myself, but I think this will reduce my stress, and my spirit could use a little uplifting! You have given me many talents. Can I use them to renew my mind and spirit? Your creativity in forming our world serves as my daily inspiration. Take away my feelings of guilt, and replace them with wondrous ideas that will lift me up and serve you. Amen.

God has given each person a storehouse of wisdom and creativity.

*Glory and honour are in his presence;
strength and gladness are in his place.*
—1 Chronicles 16:27

When we think of integrity, we think of someone who is honorable and trustworthy—a person who keeps their word and guards their reputation. To be called a woman of integrity is a high compliment. Such a person knows the difference between right and wrong and diligently pursues doing right, no matter what the obstacles. Jesus provides the best example of a person of integrity; he was not swayed by outer influences but lived a life above reproach. Integrity comes not just from the pursuit of right living, but the pursuit of God, which leads to right living.

Help me understand, Lord, that the courage I am praying for is not dry-eyed stoicism and perky denial. Courage is not hiding my feelings, even from you, and putting on a brave false face. Rather it is facing facts, weighing options, and moving ahead. No need to waste precious time pretending.

*M*y mother was a joyful person. She faced challenges like everyone else—her health in particular troubled her off and on through most of her adult life—but as a rule, she chose to focus on the positive. Her joyful outlook took many forms—she was a calm, good listener; she embraced new experiences; she was interested and interesting. And something that strikes me now is how her radiant spirit was often contagious. I myself would sometimes return from school glum or discouraged, but if we spent some quiet time together—working in the garden, say, or sometimes I would finish my homework in the kitchen while Mom cooked dinner—my own spirits lifted. Mom died last year, and as an adult, I am left to carry her bright torch for my own family. God, help me to always remember how important it is to share our joy with others so that they may experience it.

> *A*nd these things write we unto you,
> that your joy may be full.
> —1 John 1:4

$\mathcal{L}$ ord, if only all the false gods that lure us were clearly labeled. We are introduced to worldly ambition, wealth, physical perfection—any number of attractive enticements—and it isn't until we realize that the pursuit of them is using up way too much of our resources that we discover we have made these things our gods. Forgive us, Lord. Help us to keep even good things in balance and never to pursue anything with more fervor than we pursue our relationship with you.

I appreciate the connections made possible by social media, but I also recognize that like everything else, when it comes to technology, moderation is key. Yesterday I was glued to a series of screens throughout the day, from phone to laptop, and when I tore myself away to make dinner, I found myself in a particularly ill mood. While I had happily corresponded with an old friend who lives on another continent, I'd also witnessed a good deal of negativity, judgmental attitudes, and blatantly hateful behavior online. The prolonged exposure had soured my spirit, and when I snapped at my son, I realized that my choices that day did not benefit my family or me. God, help me to capitalize on the good inherent in technology, while also practicing moderation and sound judgment. Do not let me fall prey to the negativity that can be part of the online experience.

Be not deceived: evil communications corrupt good manners.
—1 Corinthians 15:33

No matter how hard I try, God of patience and support, someone finds fault with me. I am mortified about the latest criticism. I can't decide whether to run away in shame or storm back and defend my actions, for I thought I was right. Criticism hurts most when coupled with ridicule, and I feel like less of a person for the tone in which I was addressed. Give me the courage to confront this, Lord, for it is not acceptable to be treated this way even when in error. Keep me calm, factual, and open; perhaps the tone was unintentional, the critic unaware of the power of shaming. Help me remember how I feel now the next time I find fault with someone. As I've learned firsthand with you the zillions of times I messed up, there are better ways to confront mistakes than with stinging criticisms that divide and demean. Truth be known, Lord, such abrasive manners say more about the criticizer than the criticized. Keep me from passing them on.

*A*fter my first child was born, I quit my job to stay home full-time. During the first months I had moments when I felt like my intellect and some of my talents were being wasted. I longed to do something creative. At some point, though, my outlook shifted, and I came to the realization that you can find meaning in and "put something of yourself" into any task—including child care and housework. I try to look at the chores before me each day not merely as endless busywork, but as steps to providing a peaceful, orderly sanctuary where love, learning, and happiness can thrive. Thank you, Lord, for helping me find a way to put something of my very self into every task.

$\mathcal{I}$ recently turned 50 and have started to see changes in my body. I have had to start watching cholesterol levels. I've had to work harder to stay trim. Sometimes I fear that my mind is not as sharp as it once was. I don't have as great a faculty for remembering things as I did when I was younger, so I rely more on lists to keep the day running smoothly. More and more, conversations with friends circle around to these types of health issues, and sometimes I feel fearful at the prospect of aging. And yet, God reminds us that even when our bodies and minds begin to break down, he renews our spirit. God, thank you for being with me at every age, in every chapter of my life.

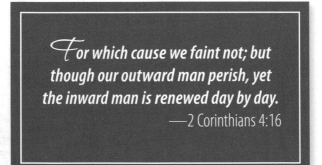

$\mathcal{F}$or which cause we faint not; but though our outward man perish, yet the inward man is renewed day by day.
—2 Corinthians 4:16

When I was a girl, my favorite uncle used to take me fishing on summer evenings when he was in town. Uncle Will was a truck driver, a job that frequently took him away from his family and friends for days at a time, and he formed some bad habits eating alone on the road. Perhaps not surprisingly, after a number of years of this, my uncle developed diabetes and high blood pressure. Will's doctor warned that his eating habits were going to kill him—a serious wake-up call that prompted some life changes. I still remember the evening my uncle and I were out on the river, hoping to catch a pike but mostly reeling in bluegills; he told me it was through God's grace that he was able to change his ways. "I'm healthier," Uncle Will said when I complimented his weight loss. And then he added something I've never forgotten: "God didn't just help me get better, he transformed me. Not just on the outside. On the inside." Lord, you are there to help us better ourselves, not just externally, but internally. Thank you for being there.

> Therefore if any man be in Christ, he is a new creature: old things are passed away; behold, all things are become new.
> —2 Corinthians 5:17

God, like snowflakes and fingerprints, you made us all different. Why would anyone want to be anyone other than who they are? What makes us unique is that special song only we can sing, and it is a song unlike any other. When combined, all of our individual songs come together in one splendid chorus! So I will sing—loud and proud!

Today, God, I will express myself authentically at every opportunity. I will be proud to be just as you made me.

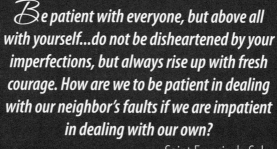

Be patient with everyone, but above all with yourself...do not be disheartened by your imperfections, but always rise up with fresh courage. How are we to be patient in dealing with our neighbor's faults if we are impatient in dealing with our own?

—Saint Francis de Sales

Chapter 13

VISUALIZE IT

*Visualize miracles,
and they will appear everywhere.
Believe in signs, and they will show
up just when you need them.
God works in mysterious ways!*

*A*nd the angel of the Lord appeared unto him in a flame of fire out of the midst of a bush: and he looked, and, behold, the bush burned with fire, and the bush was not consumed.

—Exodus 3:2

*W*ith an eye made quiet by the power of harmony and the deep power of joy, we see into the lives of things.

—William Wordsworth

$\mathcal{M}$y imagination creates a vision of what I want in my life. God then points me to the resources, people, and things I need to make that vision come alive. My only job is to have faith that all is unfolding according to his divine plans.

Inspiration is the alignment of our talents with God's purpose.

*A*nd Jesus said unto the centurion, Go thy way; and as thou hast believed, so be it done unto thee. And his servant was healed in the selfsame hour.

—Matthew 8:13

Isn't it amazing how just trusting in God's power and grace can heal us? See it, know it, and heal it. What a gift we have been given!

*Y*ou must first see in your mind's eye
what you wish to achieve.
Feel it in your heart.
Then align yourself with God's will
and go forth to achieve it,
following his inner guidance.
This is the only true secret to success!

*J*esus said unto him, If thou canst believe,
all things are possible to him that believeth.
—Mark 9:23

*D*ear God, I ask today for a bold new vision for my life. I ask for the strength and wisdom to be a better person to all those I come in contact with. I ask for the courage to step out of my comfort zone and expand my capacity for joy.

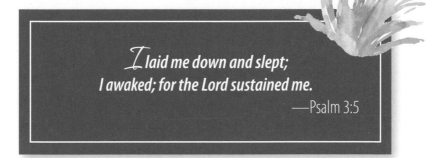

I laid me down and slept;
I awaked; for the Lord sustained me.

—Psalm 3:5

Father, right now in the middle of this trial, I feel my need for rest. Please grant me the sleep I need. May your Spirit quiet my mind and still my heart when I lie down, and chase away any distressing dreams. Let your Word fill my thoughts so that as I drift off to sleep I am surrounded by assurances of your watchful care over me. Thank you, Father, for the rest you bring even when life is at its most difficult.

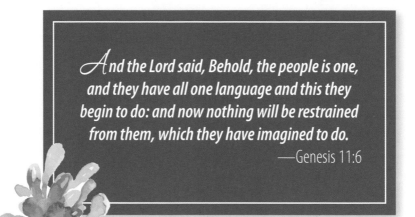

And the Lord said, Behold, the people is one, and they have all one language and this they begin to do: and now nothing will be restrained from them, which they have imagined to do.

—Genesis 11:6

You have a God-given super power,
and that power is your ability to
envision the life you wish to lead.
Use it wisely and God's blessings will unfold for you!

God, thank you for giving me this light of mine to shine. I promise never to conceal the brilliance you've bestowed upon me. May I forever reflect the glow of your loving presence. Amen.

> No man, when he hath lighted a candle, covereth it with a vessel, or putteth it under a bed; but setteth it on a candlestick, that they which enter in may see the light.
>
> —Luke 8:16

God, I ask in prayer that you help me
hold the vision of a better world,
and that I may clearly know my role
in making that better world a reality.
Let my vision join that of others,
to create a more joyful world for
those who come after us. Amen.

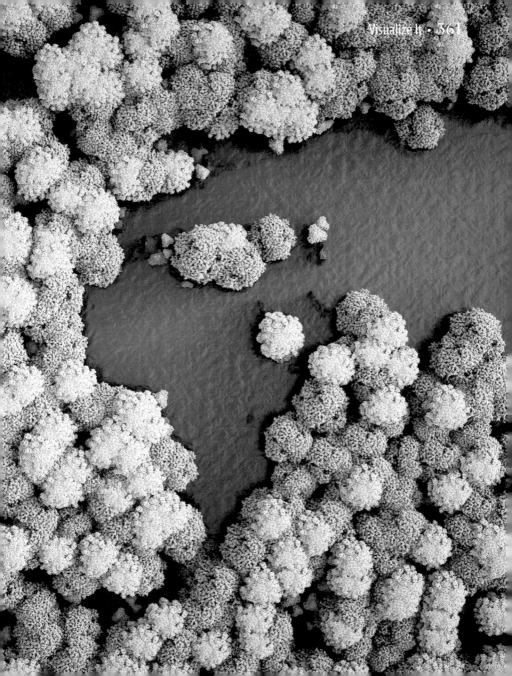

I will not let pessimists squelch my belief
that what I do can make a difference.
I am determined to maintain my
inspiration to change the world in
whatever small ways I can.

The miracle of God's presence is the vision I keep my
focus on, so that I am always striving to be better as
a person and a positive force for change. Even when
times are tough, that vision stays true, and I keep
moving towards its completion.

*G*od, when I start to feel overwhelmed
by the problems and stresses of everyday life,
I know it is time to find a quiet place where I
can retreat and rest my mind, body, and spirit.
Prayer is good for my soul. Amen.

*L*ord, I'm trying something new, and I need your strength. There are some risks involved here. I'm pushing the boundaries of my comfort zone. If this is going to succeed, I need a clear vision, extreme dedication, and about 26 hours in a day. Basically, I need divine help. Guide me in the planning. Keep me focused. Don't let me lose heart. I'm stepping forward in faith, believing that you want me to do this, but I have to admit it's more than a little terrifying. Yet I trust you. I need you. Go with me into this new enterprise. Amen.

$\mathcal{L}$ately when I lay my head on the pillow at night it is as though the curtain goes up on a horror flick: What if they give me a dreaded task at work tomorrow? What if my son fails his test? What if my dad has a nasty fall? The "what ifs" go on and on, and I wake up with even more worries on my mind. Most certainly a better way would be to start a habit of positive planning, even if just for the last five minutes before I go to bed. Maybe then I can replace my silly worries with positive hopes for the coming dawn, and I can awaken renewed, refreshed, and ready to go! Tonight, Lord, I will devote five minutes to visualizing a great tomorrow.

God, how long have I looked outside of myself for the blessings that were waiting all along? How often have I complained to you about life not being the way I wanted it when I already had what I needed to change? I now know that the blessings of prosperity and joy are all an inside job. By turning first to you, dear God, all else is then opened before me. You taught that your kingdom was within, not without, and yet once we recognized it, we would also see it all around us. Thank you, God.

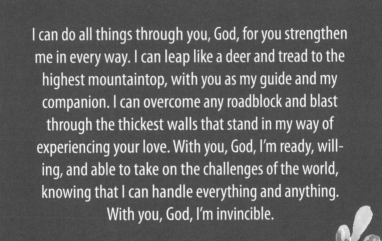

I can do all things through you, God, for you strengthen me in every way. I can leap like a deer and tread to the highest mountaintop, with you as my guide and my companion. I can overcome any roadblock and blast through the thickest walls that stand in my way of experiencing your love. With you, God, I'm ready, willing, and able to take on the challenges of the world, knowing that I can handle everything and anything. With you, God, I'm invincible.

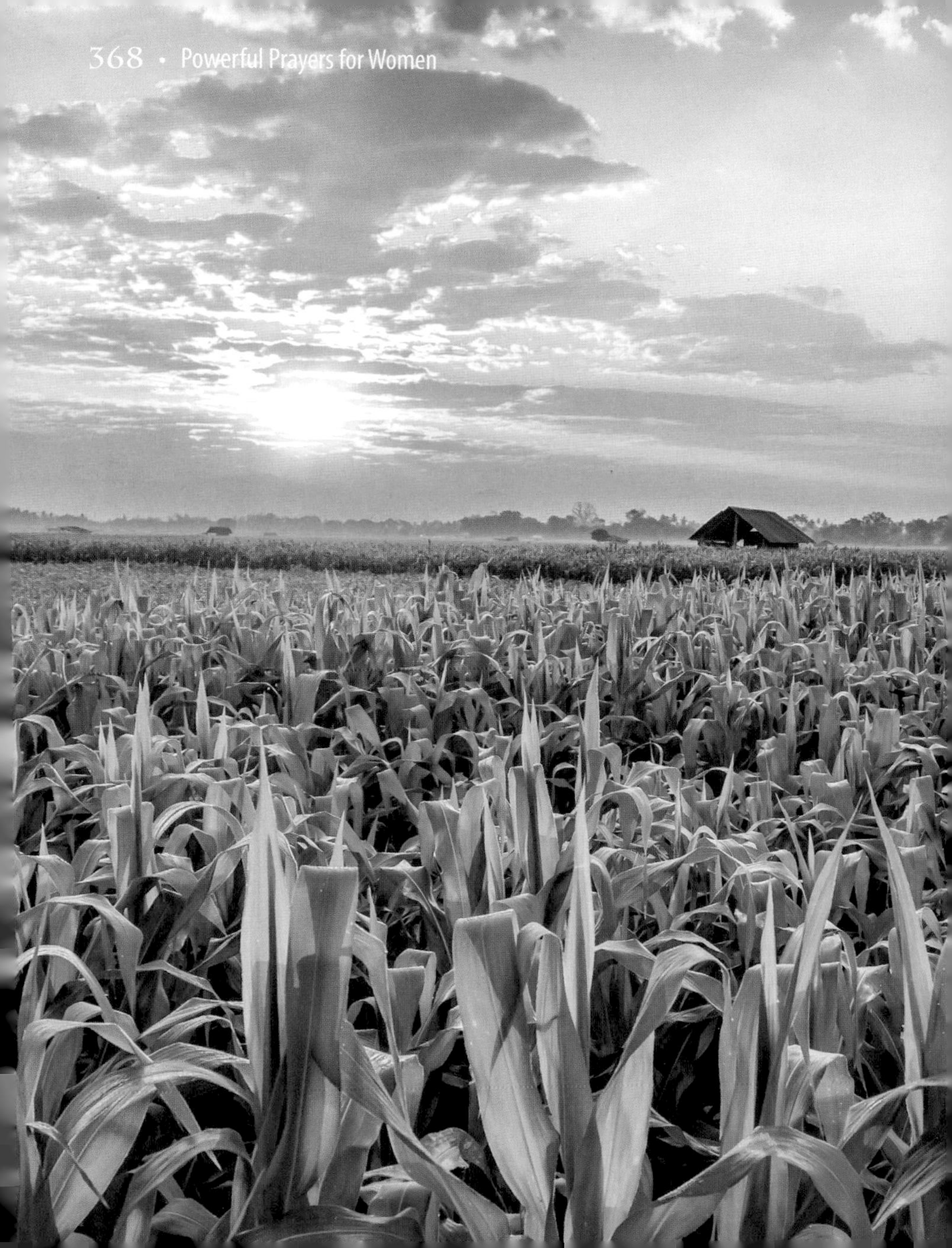

I always want to be a dreamer, O God, to feel the stir and the yearning to see my vision become reality. There are those who would say dreamers are free-floaters. When I dream I feel connected to you and to your creation, bound by purpose and a sense of call. Nourish my dreams and my striving to make them real.

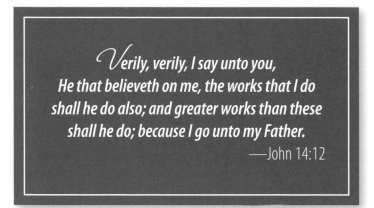

Verily, verily, I say unto you,
He that believeth on me, the works that I do
shall he do also; and greater works than these
shall he do; because I go unto my Father.

—John 14:12

You were given the dreams you dream
by a God who knew you had the
strength and fortitude to make them come true.
Go forth in his love and his belief in you.
You can do this!

There is a difference between wishing that something were so and having faith that it will be. Wishing implies an attitude of hope based on fantasy and daydreams. Faith implies an attitude of belief based upon reality and intentions. You can wish for a thing all you want, but until you have complete faith that it can—and will--be yours, it will be just a wish.

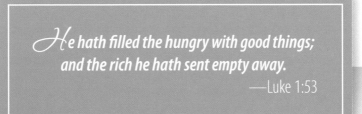

He hath filled the hungry with good things; and the rich he hath sent empty away.

—Luke 1:53

He hath made his wonderful works to be remembered:
the Lord is gracious and full of compassion.

—Psalm 111:4

To have talent and not use it is to ignore the calling of a higher voice. To be given gifts and not share them is to nullify the moving of spirit through the soul as it seeks to be made manifest in the outer world. We are given our light to let it shine, not to hide it from others for fear of drawing attention. For when we shine, we allow others to do so as well. God did not make stars in order to keep them from glowing in the night sky, nor did he make birds in order to keep them grounded. When we open our storehouse of talents and treasures, the whole world benefits and is made brighter.

$\mathcal{L}$ord, it's hard to count your blessings when all around you is chaos and despair. Though my heart is heavy and my mind cluttered, please help me to realize that before a flower can show its beauty to the sun, it first is a seed buried in the dirt. Help me to stand above the negative things in life and cast my eyes instead upon the positives that are always there, like the seedling, growing toward the moment when it will appear above ground, face to the sun.

*O*nly faith can look past a seemingly impossible situation and believe that it will change. I believe you are a God of miracles, Lord. These are days of miracles, as were the days of Noah, Moses, and Joseph. I may not see the seas parted, peoples freed, or congregations caught up to heaven, but through faith I expect wonderful gifts from you. I believe that with you, all things are possible!

> *I can do all things through Christ which strengtheneth me.*
>
> —Philippians 4:13

It is easy to have faith when things are going well, when the bills are paid and everyone is happy and in good health. But blessed is the person who has steadfast and unmoving faith when everything is going wrong. That's when faith is most needed—and least employed. If a person can suspend all intellectual judgment, look beyond the illusion of negative appearances, and believe in a Higher Power at work behind the scenes, faith will begin to move mountains, and positive solutions will appear. By putting the mighty power to work, faith will begin to work some mighty powerful miracles in your life.

But thou, O Lord, art a shield for me; my glory, and the lifter up of mine head. I cried unto the Lord with my voice, and he heard me out of his holy hill.

—Psalm 3:3–4

I am convinced that my life is not a series of random events. I believe, Father, that you are working all things together for good purposes in my life as I trust in you. And I know that includes the long, dark valleys as well as the mountaintop experiences. Of course I can always see that more clearly in retrospect, but I have learned, too, to trust that this is the case even when I am in the middle of something painful and distressing.

I see it clearly now—everything that has happened first passed
through the office of heaven and was stamped: Approved!
Therefore, I will rejoice instead of complain. I will celebrate instead
of railing against your will. If these events have a purpose,
I will seek it out. If there is a reason, I will try to find it.
I see it clearly now.

*L*ord, we want to live life to its fullest. And although we know we shouldn't place our own wants before others' wants, it is so easy to think our dreams for the future matter most. Remind us to make compromises. Our love can get us further in this life than selfishness. Amen.

$\mathcal{L}$ ast summer, my husband and I took a road trip out West. We drove from Chicago to Seattle, taking primarily two-lane roads, and making our route up as we went along. I will never forget the evening we pulled into a little town in South Dakota. It was dinnertime, that golden hour when the sunlight looks like thick yellow syrup. As we drove, the fields around us were drenched in a honey-colored light. "This must be what heaven is like," my husband remarked, nodding at a great round lake on the outskirts of town. It almost appeared to be gilded. His observation filled me with joy—and hope. I was reminded that by setting our sights on God's kingdom, we achieve a blessing in this life.

When we remember that we are working for the rewards of heaven, we are able to persevere through the tasks ahead of us. Thank you, Lord, for making the things of heaven available to those who seek them.

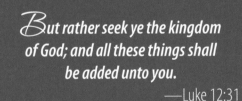

But rather seek ye the kingdom of God; and all these things shall be added unto you.

—Luke 12:31

When your dreams seem unreachable, trust that
God will lighten your burdens, smooth your path,
and urge you on to a brighter tomorrow.

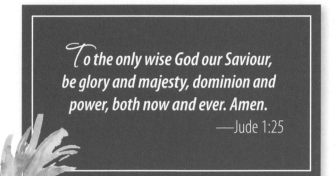

To the only wise God our Saviour, be glory and majesty, dominion and power, both now and ever. Amen.

—Jude 1:25

Holy God, you have shown me light and life. You are stronger than any natural power. Accept the words from my heart that struggle to reach you. Accept the silent thoughts and feelings that are offered to you. Clear my mind of the clutter of useless facts. Bend down to me, and lift me in your arms. Make me holy as you are holy. Give me a voice to sing of your love to others. Amen.

Take time to work—
It is the price of success.
Take time to think—
It is the source of power.
Take time to play—
It is the secret of perpetual youth.
Take time to read—
It is the fountain of wisdom.
Take time to be friendly—
It is the road to happiness.
Take time to dream—
It is hitching your wagon to a star.
Take time to love and be loved—
It is the privilege of the gods.
Take time to look around—
It is too short a day to be selfish.
Take time to laugh—
It is music to the soul.

—Anonymous